Christian Braun

Fitness for Fighters

Meyer & Meyer Sport

ANDOVER COLLEGE

Original title: Fitness für Fighter
© Meyer & Meyer Verlag, 2009

British Library Cataloguing in Publication Data
A catalogue record for this book is available from the British Library

Fitness for Fighters
Christian Braun
Maidenhead: Meyer & Meyer Sport (UK) Ltd., 2010
ISBN: 978-1-84126-279-6

© 2010 by Meyer & Meyer Sport (UK) Ltd.
Aachen, Adelaide, Auckland, Budapest, Cape Town, Graz, Indianapolis,
Maidenhead, Olten (CH), Singapore, Toronto
Member of the World
Sport Publishers' Association (WSPA)
www.w-s-p-a.org
Printed by: B.O.S.S Druck und Medien GmbH
ISBN: 978-1-84126-279-6
E-Mail: info@m-m-sports.com
www.m-m-sports.com

Fitness for Fighters

Warning:

This book contains some techniques that can be very dangerous and must only be practiced under the supervision of a qualified trainer or instructor. The author and the publisher cannot be held responsible for any injuries that might occur.

For reasons of simplicity, this book has been written using exclusively the male form of the personal pronoun. Of course, this should be understood to include the female form as well.

Index

Foreword

Since 1982, I have been regularly taking part in martial arts training at least four times a week. During this time, what I will call 'workout and cool down' training has not changed that much. Traditional warm-up training continues to consist of strength training without equipment and the cool down of *stretching* exercises.

About 20 years ago, martial arts followers like us did our warm-ups to music. We listened to Rock music because at that time Techno music had not yet appeared. At that time I wrote to various TV stations suggesting that, instead of – to my mind – rather boring 15-minute early morning gymnastic programs, they should have a mix of martial arts techniques to music. Unfortunately, this was turned down. A few years later, another martial arts follower – Billy Blanks – was very successful with this.

I don't say this to claim that I was the inventor of this kind of training, today called by various names – Tai-Bo, Tae Bo©, Ju-Jutsu-Robics . . . Lots of martial arts followers trained then and still train to music.

After several years of the traditional warm-up training using push-ups, sit-ups and knee bends, I have moved away from this concept by using the actual techniques themselves as warm-up training right from the beginning, albeit in a reduced form of intensity. For example, I also often use punching and kicking techniques with a punch mitt. Carried out slowly and in a controlled fashion, the body is warmed up and the time can be used more effectively to train for the techniques. A suitable intensity can be selected that gives the cardiovascular system a workout as well.

In order for the training not to be boring, I also include occasional games for the warm-up training. They keep the motivation up and are much more fun than the older drills we used.

Before and following training, it is recommended that the athlete performs stretching exercises, particularly for the muscle groups that will be used and put under strain.

In most training rooms there are no machines or weights lying around like you see in a fitness studio. I have built this book on the premise that no equipment is needed other than a few aids (such as skipping ropes, belts, punch mitts and a resistance exercise band) as well as a punch bag.

All the points covered above are also described in this book. I have intentionally avoided including a large theory section about strength training and a section about dietary needs in this book, because sufficient literature is available covering these topics. This book is suitable for every athlete who, for example, wants to train at home or when in a hotel, or alternatively for those who want to assemble a catalog of exercises to use in his warm-up and workout training.

Acknowledgements

I would like to thank my students Martin Liebel, Christian Gumbinger, my friend and student Gunther Hatzenbühler and my student and partner Gabriele Rogall-Zelt for their support in writing this book.

Martin Liebel

Christian Gumbinger

Gunther Hatzenbühler

Gabriele Rogall-Zelt

I   The Theoretical Section

1   How the Muscles Work

Our muscles are made up of many individual muscle fibers which are instructed to contract by the brain. Thus it is possible for us to be able to lift different weights. The muscle contraction is controlled by the brain and only those muscles are used that are needed to lift the various weights.

This is why a trained muscle works more economically than an untrained one. For example, if we want to bend the upper arm, the bicep tendon is anchored to the bone of the lower arm. To stretch the arm, the triceps – i.e., the antagonist counteracted by the agonist – is activated.

There are two different ways of working that differentiate between muscles. In a **static** loading, a muscle is contracted without its length altering. This kind of contraction comes into play in **isometric training** and this is described later in this book. Then there is the **dynamic** loading that takes place positively, i.e. the muscle shortens or negatively, i.e. the muscle lengthens.

In the actual training, this means that when a weight is lifted, positive dynamics are used and when the weight is lowered down, negative dynamics are used.

An example of this is a fist punch. The punching action, i.e. stretching out the arm, is a negative dynamic action, while pulling the arm back is a positive dynamic action. In order to use a punch successfully when fighting someone, you need not only **strength** but also **agility**, **speed**, **stamina** and **coordination**. These five terms comprise the capabilities of the motor system.

2   The Capabilities of the Motor System

The motor system consists of the following capabilities:

- Stamina
- Agility
- Coordination
- Strength
- Speed

Strength can be further divided into the following types:

- Sustained Strength (Endurance)
- Maximum Strength
- Speed Strength
- Reaction Strength

2.1   Maximum Strength

The term **maximum strength** means the total strength that can be freely exerted against a resistance. To improve maximum strength, the following factors must be trained for:

Intramuscular coordination
Intermuscular coordination
Muscle cross-sectional size

Maximum strength is also called basic strength. It consists of the following strength groups:

- Endurance
- Speed strength
- Reaction strength

2.2   Endurance

Endurance is a mixture of strength and stamina. It should enable the athlete to achieve his highest performance over the longest possible time. Training for this consists of a limited intensity of approximately 30-50 % of the maximum strength with high repeat frequency (15-30), dependent on the intensity.

2.3   Speed Strength

Speed strength is defined as the ability to build up maximum strength in speed and execute a movement in the shortest possible time. Speed strength consists of:

- Start Force
- Exclusive Force

In most forms of the martial arts, kicks and punches have to be performed in the shortest possible time. The start force is the power used in beginning the movement or action. The exclusive force is the increase in power that is achieved on the way to the target.

2.4   Reaction Strength

Reaction strength describes the ability of the muscles in a reactive movement, i.e. to enable a highly powerful hit during the muscle shortening cycle of stretching. It can also be likened to a special form of speed strength.

2.5   Training Frequency

"Once is better than nothing at all!" With beginners, one can already tell a difference in progress with a training frequency of once a week. However, training two times would be better. Top athletes, of course, have to train considerably more often. They have to take care to allow time for the muscle groups trained to recover. Dependent on intensity and the particular muscle group, it can take up to three days for full recovery.

2.6   When to Set the Next Training Goals

After a training session our bodies go about the business of replenishing our reserves so as to achieve a balance between our level of performance and the efforts required to achieve that level. This is done by the body adapting itself to a higher level of reserves (called **supercompensation**). For the recovery process to be successful the body needs between one and three days (dependent on the training intensity and muscle group used). We always use our legs, so the leg muscles regenerate quicker than, for example, the lower back muscles. Once the body has regenerated to a higher level than before, this is the moment to set the next training goal. If no further training goal is set within 2 to 3 days, then the additional reserves that have been built up will, in general no longer be available after a week. Therefore, the new training session should begin within 2 to 3 days. However, the next training session shouldn't be planned too early, because the reserves will not have been built up sufficiently and in such cases there is a danger of losing the training value to the body.

Because of this factor, it makes sense in daily training to alternate between the muscle groups being exercised.

2.7   Specific Warm-up Exercises

Concerning the actual technique that you are planning to train with, you must warm up and do stretching exercises with the appropriate muscle group. You must avoid pulling a muscle or causing any damage to the muscle fibers. Once you have done the warm-up, then the first technique exercises should be done with limited intensity.

2.8   Cooling Down

After the training you should do body stretching exercises. These help the regeneration process in the body. Cooling down is as important as warming up. During the cool down phase, the body throws off any waste energy. This subject is covered in more detail at the end of this book.

II   The Practical Section

1   Solo Training

1.1   Isometric Training

About 25 years ago there was a classified ad in a journal about a book claiming "5 % more power in 7 days." I found the title interesting and I ordered the book. The book went into tension exercises for the various different muscle groups in the body. The idea was that you had to tense the muscles for a certain length of time (a few seconds). You began with the arm muscles and finished off with the calf muscles.

You were supposed to do the exercises every day. For a time, I did this, but I couldn't keep a routine going. Even today, I still occasionally do them. This is mainly when I am at work on the road and spending nights in a hotel. I really believe that these exercises can help build up the muscles and give you more power. However, I have to say that, in my opinion, they only work to a small degree.

Where you have injured a bone, this sort of exercise can be used to reduce the loss of muscle power while it heals. Once I had my metatarsus in plaster for several weeks. During this time, I kept tensing the muscles in my thigh and kept it relatively fit despite the injury and lack of normal movement of the muscle.

Nowadays, there are several TV commercials that show a type of stomach trainer that is strapped to the tensed stomach muscles in order to encourage muscle growth. The exercise certainly encourages muscle growth, but the equipment is easily replaced by other much cheaper aids. You could use all sorts of objects to achieve the same result: for example, you could press a book to the stomach. The same result can be achieved by sitting and tensing the stomach muscles, and holding them tensed for a time. This kind of training is called *isometric training*. This has been researched and developed since 1953 by Prof. Hettinger.

1.1.1 'What's Special about Isometric Training?'

1. For most of the exercises, no equipment is required. For some of the exercises, it helps if you use a hand towel, resistance exercise band, skipping rope or an object in the room such as a chair or the wall, etc.

2. To get the muscle to increase in size, only a few seconds (at least 3 seconds) of full tensing of the muscle is needed. For this you need no dumbbell or equipment such as the kind you find in a fitness studio.

3. In isometric training, many muscle fibers respond at the same time, while in conventional strength training (also with equipment) the same result is hardly achieved. In conventional training, a muscle must remain under a maximum of 50 % loading for about 20 seconds in order to encourage an increase in muscle size.

4. In conventional strength training, several repeats of sets are carried out. This is not necessary in isometric training. Thus the time spent is considerably less than in conventional training.

5. This kind of training is also suitable for older people and for people with cardiovascular complaints, because it does not tax the cardiovascular system. However, care must be taken not to carry out exercises when the strain causes the exerciser to hold his breath for periods of time.

1.1.2 'Why Doesn't Isometric Training Achieve Total Success?'

On the one hand, isometric exercise does not train the cardiovascular system as claimed by many athletes. On the other hand, beginners often make the mistake of doing the exercises straining and not breathing. This can lead to high blood pressure and circulatory problems. In a worse case, straining and not breathing can even cause you to lose consciousness.

Furthermore, this sort of exercise does not train the neuromuscular interplay (coordination). It is therefore recommended that dynamic exercise forms are also used. It would be a good idea to follow up a session of isometric exercises with a session of dynamic exercises. You will find dynamic exercises for the individual muscle groups listed in this book.

1.1.3   Correct Breathing While Exercising

In order to avoid straining and not breathing, it is recommended that you carry out balanced breathing in and out before undergoing the exercise and then continue this rhythm during the exercise. Breathing plays no part in the exercise.

1.1.4   Workout

The Lower Arms
1. Roll up a hand towel and gripping it very tightly in both hands, hold it out at arm's length. Hold the tension for 15 seconds.

The Upper Arms
Biceps
1. Bend the arm at the elbow and tense the biceps as hard as you can, holding it for 15 seconds.

So that the biceps take on a finer form, you can extend the exercise as follows:
1. Bend the arm . . .
2. . . . turn the open hand so that the little finger is in a counterclockwise direction. Tense the biceps as hard as you can and hold the tension for 15 seconds.

Triceps
1. Let your arms hang down loosely by your sides.
2. Clench your fists.
3. Pull both arms to the rear so that the triceps are tensed. Tense the triceps as hard as you can and hold this for 15 seconds.

Neck

Pull the shoulders up in a shrugging motion and tense the neck, holding it for 15 seconds.

Shoulders

1. Stretch the arms out sideways with the palms of the hands facing the ceiling. Pull the arms backwards and upwards at an angle of 45°.
2. Stretch the arms out sideways with the palms of the hands facing the floor. Pull the arms backwards and upwards at an angle of 45°.

3. Stretch the arms out sideways with the palms of the hands facing forwards. Pull the arms backwards and upwards at an angle of 45°.
4. Stretch the arms out sideways with the palms of the hands facing rearwards. Pull the arms backwards and upwards at an angle of 45°.

Back

Hollow your back. Tense the lower muscles of the back and hold for 15 seconds.

Chest Muscles

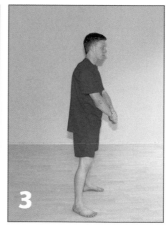

1. Take hold of your right wrist with your left hand and lift the arms up to head height. Press your hands down in the direction of the floor thus tensing the upper chest muscles.
2. Take hold of your right wrist with your left hand and lift the arms up to chest height. Press your hands down in the direction of the floor thus tensing the middle chest muscles.
3. Take hold of your right wrist with your left hand and lift the arms up to stomach height. Press your hands down in the direction of the floor thus tensing the lower chest muscles.

4. Press your palms together and push them hard together thus tensing your chest muscles.

5. Hook a finger of the right hand around a finger of the left hand. Pull the arms outwards thus tensing the chest muscles.

Latissimus

1. Place both of your hands on your partner's shoulders. Tense your Latissimus and hold for 15 seconds.

2. Place both of your hands on your partner's elbows. Tense your Latissimus and hold for 15 seconds.

Stomach
Bend the upper body forwards. Tense your stomach muscles and hold for 15 seconds.

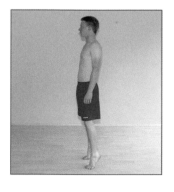

Buttocks
Lift up onto the balls of the feet. Tense your buttocks and hold for 15 seconds.

Thighs
Alternately, lift the legs up and stretch them out tensing and holding the thigh muscle for 15 seconds.

Calves
Turn the calf of the leg outwards and place the leg on the ball of the foot, tensing and holding the calf muscle for 15 seconds.

Shinbone
Lift your leg up and tense the side muscle of the shinbone, holding it for 15 seconds.

1.2   Running and Jumping Jacks

Running is an ideal way of warming up. As soon as the first drops of sweat appear on the forehead, you can start doing strengthening exercises or movement forms/drills.

It should be possible for a follower of martial arts to run continuously for 30 minutes. For this, the speed must be chosen that allows him to be able to speak three sentences at a time. At this speed he is running well over the fat burning rate and into an energy-gaining zone. He is running in the aerobic zone. It is ideal if you can run in the open air next to nature, as this not only allows you to do stamina training but also helps you to relax. Make sure you have the correct footwear. Dependent on the surface (forest floor or concrete) and your weight (above or below 80 kg) special shoes may be needed. This is necessary to avoid damaging the joints, particularly for heavier runners.

When buying the appropriate footwear, make sure you are being served by a qualified salesperson. In a good store, your running style can be captured on video (showing how your foot falls while running) and the specialist salesperson can analyze it and find you the correct shoes.

If it is not possible at the beginning for you to run continuously for 30 minutes, then break the time up with small pauses. Try to reduce these pauses every time you train until you can run the full 30 minutes. Make sure you always have enough breath to be able to speak. If you are struggling for air and cannot speak, then reduce the running speed until you are able to do these things without a problem. You will be more successful this way.

1.2.1   In a Circle

• Forwards

• Backwards

• Crossing over the legs

• On one leg

• With legs together

- Hopping forwards

- Hopping backwards

- Changing direction on command

- On command, carry out the following exercises:

  - Lie down on the stomach

  - Lie down on the back

  - Do a push-up

  - Do a forward roll

  - Do a backward roll

  - Fall forwards

  - Fall backwards

  - . . .

1.2.2   Standing

- Marching on the spot

- Lunge step to one side

- Go forward with feet in V form

- In a fighting stance backwards and forwards

- Changing position

- Take step forwards

- Take a step sideways

- Take a step backwards

- Bend the knees and then kick forward with one leg

- Bend the knees and then kick sideways with one leg

- Jump up stretched in the air

- Jump up in the air and then down to do push-ups

1.2.3 Jumping Jacks

Exercise 1

  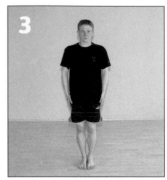

1. Start position.

2. Open the legs wider and at the same time lift the arms upwards from the sides.

3. Now bring the legs together and the arms down again.

Exercise 2

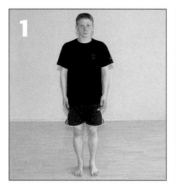  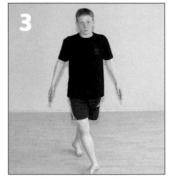

1. Start position.

2. Open the legs wider and at the same time lift the arms upwards from the sides.

3. Now cross the legs so that the right leg is in front and at the same time bring the arms down again.

4. Open the legs wider and at the same time lift the arms upwards from the sides.

5. Now cross the legs so that the left leg is in front and at the same time bring the arms down again.

Exercise 3

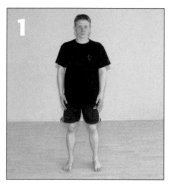

1. Start position.

2. Open the legs wider and at the same time lift the arms up to shoulder height from the sides.

3. Now bring the legs together and the arms forward until the palms touch each other.

Exercise 4

1. Start position.

2. Open the legs wider and at the same time lift the arms up to shoulder height from the sides with the palms of the hands facing forwards.

3. Now cross the legs so that the right leg is in front and at the same time bring the arms forward until the palms of the hands touch each other.

4. Open the legs wide again and at the same time lift the arms upwards to shoulder height from the sides.

5. Now cross the legs so that the left leg is in front and at the same time bring the arms forward until the palms of the hands touch each other.

Exercise 5

1. Start position.

2. Open the legs wider and at the same time lift the arms up to shoulder height from the sides with the palms of the hands facing downwards.

3. Now close the legs again and at the same time bring the arms forward until you can cross them over each other.

4. Open the legs wide again and at the same time lift the arms upwards to shoulder height from the outside. The palms of the hands are facing downwards.

Exercise 6

1. Start position.

2. Open the legs wider and at the same time lift the arms up to shoulder height from the outsides with the palms of the hands facing forwards.

3. Now cross the legs so that the right leg is forward and at the same time bring the arms forward until they cross each other. The palms of the hands are facing downwards.

4. Open the legs wider and at the same time lift the arms up to shoulder height from the outsides with the palms of the hands facing forwards.

5. Now cross the legs so that left leg is forward and at the same time bring the arms forward until they cross each other. The palms of the hands are facing downwards.

6. Open the legs wide again and at the same time lift the arms upwards to shoulder height from the sides.

Exercise 7

1. Start position.
2. Take a lunge step forward with the right leg leaving the left leg to the rear. At the same time stretch the right arm forwards and upwards while the left arm is stretched out to the rear and downwards.
3. Now bring the right leg to the rear and place the left leg forward in a lunge step. Stretch the right arm downwards to the rear while the left arm is stretched out forwards and upwards.

Exercise 8

1. Start position.
2. Take a lunge step forwards with the right leg leaving the left leg to the rear and bring the arms sideways and upwards over the head.
3. Change the lunge legs and now bring the arms down out to the sides.

Exercise 9

1. Start position.

2. Take a lunge step forwards with the right leg leaving the left leg to the rear and bring the arms sideways to shoulder height with the palms of the hands facing forwards.

3. Change the lunge legs and now bring the arms forward so that the palms of the hands are touching.

4. Take a lunge step forwards with the right leg and leave the left leg to the rear bringing the arms outstretched at shoulder height with the palms of hands facing forwards.

Exercise 10

1. Start position.

2. Take a lunge step forwards with the right leg leaving the left leg to the rear and bring the arms sideways to shoulder height with the palms of the hands facing downwards.

3. Change the lunge legs and now bring the arms forward so that they are crossing over each other.

4. Take a lunge step forwards with the right leg and leave the left leg to the rear bringing the arms outstretched at shoulder height with the palms of hands facing downwards.

5. Now take a lunge step rearwards with the right leg and a lunge step forwards with the left leg. Bring the arms forward until they are crossed over each other.

Exercise 11

1. Start position.

2. Open the legs wider and at the same time lift the right arm upwards and bring the left arm to the side stretched downwards.

3. Now close the legs and bring the right arm downwards stretched down the side and bring the left arm upwards.

4. Open the legs wider and bring the stretched right arm upwards and the stretched left arm downwards.

Exercise 12

1. Start position.

2. Open the legs to one side and at the same time take a lunge step 45° forward to the right and lift the arms up over the head from the sides.

3. Now jump back into the start position.

4. Open the legs to one side and at the same time take a lunge step 45° forward to the left and lift the arms up over the head from the sides.

5. Now jump back into the start position again.

1.3　Rope Skipping

You can vary the load on yourself dependent on the speed that you skip with the rope. You can also vary the intensity as you do the exercise.

Example:
1.　Start with 30 seconds of slow skipping.

2.　Then do 30 seconds skipping fast.

3.　Then do 30 seconds skipping slowly again.

You can use the following variations:
* Skip with the feet closed
* Run on the spot hardly lifting the feet from the ground
* Run on the spot but this time lifting the legs up high
* Skip forwards
* Skip backwards
* Alternately skip with the feet pointing forwards
* Alternately skip with a foot out to the side
* Cross over the rope as you skip
* Swing the rope twice to one skipping step

1.4   Punchbag Training

1.4.1   The Correct Punchbag

Before you practice punchbag techniques you must chose the correct punchbag. The following are materials that can be used:

- Cloth
- Plastic/Artificial leather (Vinyl)
- Leather

The punchbag made of leather and filled with sand is the most expensive of them all but has a longer life. When using a bag made of cloth or artificial material make sure you wear hand protectors otherwise you will soon find you are damaging the skin of your knuckles. The sack filling is also important.

You can use the following materials:
- Sawdust
- Strips of cloth
- Sand

When the sack is filled with sand, it will be very heavy and extremely hard. This will very quickly cause damage to your hands. A bag that is not well sewn can allow sawdust to spew out when struck. This is not good for the person practicing as it pollutes the air and gets up the nose causing you to sneeze. I personally prefer to use a sack filled with cloth pieces. The sack is not heavy and everything stays inside the sack. You can buy the sack with or without a filling. The shipment of a filled sack will cost a lot more than one that is empty. Despite this I would recommend buying a filled sack. If you want to fill the sack yourself then the best place to find pieces of cloth is your local tailor's shop.

The hanging attachment is also important. The sack should be able to swivel around. A suitable device to use to hang it from can be found in a shop selling building equipment.

You should also consider how long the sack should be. It should be at least 120 cm long. If you going to practice lowkicks then I recommend a sack that is about 180 cm long.

Before you start training with a punchbag you should mark off the various heights of head, stomach and knees (i.e., for a long bag) with tape. You should always imagine that you are striking an opponent and not just a bag when you are performing your punching and kicking techniques.

1.4.2   How to Correctly Form a Fist

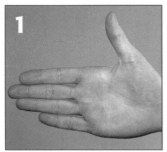

1.   Open the hand.
2.   Roll the fingers in.
3.   Place the thumb along the center parts of the fingers.

The fist can be used horizontally, vertically or at an angle of 45°.

1.4.3   How to Cover the Head with the Correct Guard

1.   Let you arms hang outstretched down close by your sides.
2.   Bend your arms at the elbows so that the fists cover your face and your elbows cover your liver and spleen.

1.4.4   How to Punch Correctly

Punches at the Head

1. If you are right-handed then you stand with your left leg forward. The weight of your body is equally placed over both legs. The heel of the rear leg is raised up.
2. The punch stems from the leg and then the hip is pushed forward...
3. ... followed by the shoulder and then the elbow...
4. ... ending up with the punch being delivered. Be sure that the back of the hand is directly in line with the lower arm, otherwise you can hurt your wrist. If you already have experience in the martial arts, then you can use the knuckle of the forefinger and middle finger (e.g., as a Karateka). Other martial arts followers (e.g., Wing Tsun) use the ring finger to hit with. For beginners, I recommend they use the striking surface of the whole of the knuckles of the hand. When delivering the punch, the head is dropped down until the chin almost touches the breastbone. The chin is covered by the upper arm.
5. The arm is then pulled back at the same speed as used for the delivery.

Punches at the Upper Body (Stomach)

1. If you are right-handed then you stand with your left leg forward. The weight of your body is equally placed over both legs. The heel of the rear leg is raised up.

2. Bend your knees and lower your body. The punch stems from the leg and the right knee twists inwards with the hips then being pushed forward followed by the shoulders and then the elbow ending up with the delivery of the punch. Be sure that the back of the hand is directly in line with the lower arm otherwise you can hurt your wrist. If you already have experience in the martial arts, then you can use the knuckle of the forefinger and middle finger (e.g., as a Karateka). Other martial arts followers (e.g., Wing Tsun) use the ring finger to hit with. For beginners, I recommend they use the striking surface of the whole of the knuckles of the hand. When delivering the punch, the head is dropped down until the chin almost touches the breastbone. The chin is covered by the upper arm.

    The arm is then pulled back at the same speed as used for the delivery.

1.4.5 Punching and Kicking Techniques with the Hanging Punchbag

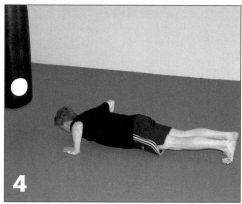

The exercise should be done for 2 min. followed by a pause of about 1 min.

1.-2. Stand in front of the punchbag carrying out rapid short jabbing hits for 10 seconds, with at the same time rapid steps on the spot.

3.-5. Drop down into the push-up position and do a push-up.

1. Stand in front of the punchbag with the left foot forward . . .

2. . . . and lower the body . . .

3. . . . delivering a punch with the right arm (cross) at the punchbag.

4. Then return to the starting position.

1. Stand in front of the punchbag . . .
2. . . . and deliver a jabbing punch at the punchbag with the left hand . . .
3. . . . then pull the left arm back . . .
4. . . . and deliver another jabbing punch . . .
5. . . . pulling the left arm back again.
6. Now deliver a cross punch with the right hand . . .
7. . . . and pull the right arm back . . .
8. . . . and follow this up with another cross punch with the right hand . . .
9. . . . and pull the right arm back.

1. Stand at kicking distance in front of the punchbag . . .

2. . . . and, beginning with the left foot, take a gliding step forwards and anchor the left leg, delivering at the same time a left-handed jab at head height.

3. Now take a gliding step backwards with the right foot.

1. Stand at kicking distance in front of the punchbag . . .

2. . . . and, beginning with the left foot, take a gliding step forwards and anchor the left leg, delivering at the same time a right-handed cross at head height.

3. Now take a gliding step backwards with the right foot.

1. Stand at kicking distance in front of the punchbag . . .

2. . . . and, beginning with the left foot, take a gliding step forwards and anchor the left leg . . .

3. . . . delivering at the same time a left-handed swinging punch (hook) at head height.

4. Now take a gliding step backwards with the right foot.

1. Stand at kicking distance in front of the punchbag...

2. ...and, beginning with the left foot, take a gliding step forwards and anchor the left leg, delivering at the same time a right-handed uppercut at head height.

3. Now take a gliding step backwards with the right foot.

1. Stand in front of the punchbag...

2. ...and hold it firmly in both hands bringing the left leg to the rear...

3. ...and deliver a strike with the left knee at the punchbag...

4. . . . and then placing the right leg to the rear . . .

5. . . . deliver a strike with the right knee at the punchbag.

1. Stand at kicking distance in front of the punchbag . . .

2. . . . and, beginning with the left foot, take a gliding step forwards and anchor the left leg, delivering at the same time a left-handed jab at head height . . .

3. . . . followed by a right-handed cross at stomach height . . .

4. . . . and then a left-handed jab at head height.

5. Now take a gliding step backwards with the right foot.

1. Stand at kicking distance in front of the punchbag . . .

2. . . . and, beginning with the left foot, take a gliding step forwards and anchor the left leg, delivering at the same time a left-handed jab at head height . . .

3. . . . followed by a right-handed cross at stomach height . . .

4. . . . and then a left-handed hook at head height . . .

5. . . . and then a right-handed cross at head height.

6. Now take a gliding step backwards with the right foot.

1. Stand at kicking distance in front of the punchbag...

2. ...and, beginning with the left foot, take a gliding step forwards and anchor the left leg, delivering at the same time a right-handed cross at head height...

3. ...followed by a left-handed uppercut at head height...

4. ...and then a right-handed cross at stomach height.

5. Now take a gliding step backwards with the right foot.

1. Stand with the left leg forwards and lift the left hand up forwards (with the object of disturbing the opponent's sight) . . .

2. . . . and deliver a right-handed cross at stomach height . . .

3. . . . followed by a left-handed hook at the liver . . .

4. . . . and then a strike with the right elbow at the head.

5. Now take a gliding step backwards with the right foot.

1. Stand with the left leg forwards . . .

2. . . . and take a step out to the side with the left leg and deliver a left-handed hook at stomach height . . .

3. . . . and then deliver a left-handed hook at head height . . .

4. . . . followed by a right-handed hook at head height . . .

5. Now take a gliding step backwards with the right foot.

1. Stand with the left leg forwards . . .

2. . . . and take a step out to the side with the left leg and deliver a left-handed hook at stomach height . . .

3. . . . and then deliver a right-handed hook at stomach height . . .

4. . . . followed by a left-handed uppercut at head height . . .

5. . . . and a strike with the right elbow at head height.

6. Now take a gliding step backwards with the right foot.

1. Stand with the left leg forwards . . .
2. . . . and deliver a semi-circular kick with the right leg at upper body/head height . . .
3. . . . followed by a left-handed jab at head height . . .
4. . . . and then deliver a right-handed cross at stomach height . . .
5. . . . and a lowkick with the left leg at the opponent's leg height . . .
6. . . . followed up with a semi-circular kick with the right leg at the upper body/head.
7. Now take a gliding step backwards with the right foot.

1. Stand with the left leg forwards ...
2. ... and then take a step with the left leg to the rear and place the right leg forwards at an angle of at least 90° to the punchbag ...
3. ... and deliver a left-legged lowkick at the opponent's leg height.
4. This is followed with a right-handed cross at head height ...
5. ... and then a left-handed hook at stomach height ...
6. ... and a right-handed cross at head height ...
7. ... and finally a semi-circular kick with the right leg at the opponent's ribs.
8. Now take a gliding step backwards with the right foot.

1. Stand with the left leg forwards . . .

2. . . . and deliver a knee-up kick with the left knee at stomach height.

3. Now deliver an elbow strike with the right arm forwards at head height . . .

4. . . . followed by a left-handed uppercut at head height . . .

5. . . . and then deliver a right-handed cross at head height . . .

6. Now take a gliding step backwards with the right foot.

1. Stand with the left leg forwards . . .
2. . . . and then take a step with the right leg to the right so that the right leg is at an angle of at least 90° to the punchbag . . .
3. . . . and deliver a left-legged highkick (semi-circular) at head height.
4. This is followed with a right-handed cross at head height . . .
5. . . . and then a left-handed uppercut at head height . . .
6. . . . and a right-handed cross at head height . . .
7. . . . and a left-legged lowkick . . .
8. . . . and finally a semi-circular highkick with the right leg at stomach height.
9. Now take a gliding step backwards with the right foot.

1. Stand with the left leg forwards ...

2. ... and deliver a left-handed jab at head height ...

3. ... and a right-handed cross at head height ...

4. ... and then deliver a left-legged lowkick at the opponent's leg height

5. ... and a semi-circular highkick with the right leg at stomach height

6. Now take a gliding step backwards with the right foot.

1. Stand with the left leg forwards...

2. ...and then take a lunge step with the right leg to the right so that the right leg is at an angle of at least 90° to the punchbag...

3. ...and deliver a left-legged lowkick at the opponent's leg height.

4. This is followed with a right-handed cross at head height...

5. ...and then a left-handed hook at head height...

6. ...and a further right-handed cross at stomach height...

7. ...and finally a semi-circular highkick with the left leg at stomach height.

8. Now take a gliding step backwards with the right foot.

1. Stand with the left leg forwards . . .
2. . . . and deliver a right-legged lowkick at the opponent's leg height.
3. Deliver a left-handed jabbing punch at head height . . .
4. . . . and a right-handed cross at head height . . .
5. . . . and a left-legged lowkick at the opponent's leg height.
6. Finally, deliver a semi-circular highkick with the right leg at stomach height.
7. Now take a gliding step backwards with the right foot.

1. Stand with the left leg forwards ...
2. ... and deliver a left-handed jab at head height ...
3. ... then a right-handed cross at head height ...
4. ... followed by a left-handed hook at stomach height ...
5. ... then a further right-handed cross at head height.
6. Place the right leg to the rear and deliver a left-legged lowkick at the opponent's legs ...
7. ... and then place the left leg to the rear and deliver a semi-circular highkick at head height.
8. Now take a gliding step backwards with the right foot.

1. Stand with the left leg forwards . . .
2. . . . and deliver a left-legged lowkick at the opponent's legs . . .
3. . . . followed by a strike with the right elbow at head height . . .
4. . . . and then a left-handed hook at head height . . .
5. . . . and a right-handed cross at head height.
6. . . . ending the combination with a semi-circular kick at stomach height with the left leg.
7. Now take a gliding step backwards with the right foot.

1.4.6　Punching and Kicking Techniques at a Punchbag on the Ground

Do these drills for 2 minutes and repeat 3-5 times.

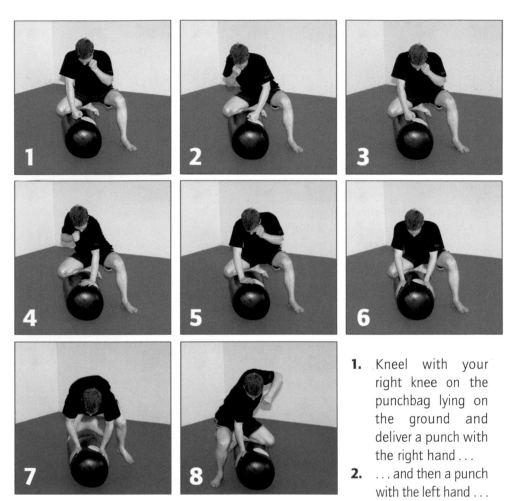

1. Kneel with your right knee on the punchbag lying on the ground and deliver a punch with the right hand . . .
2. . . . and then a punch with the left hand . . .
3. . . . followed by another punch with the right hand.
4. The punchbag is now struck using the heel of the open hand – first the left hand . . .
5. . . . then the heel of the open right hand.
6. Place both hands on the punchbag . . .
7. . . . and jump over it . . .
8. . . . this time, place the left knee on the punchbag and start going through the same combination of strikes as above from the other side.

1

2

3

4

5

6

7

1. Sit on the punchbag lying on the ground.
2. Deliver an open-handed strike with the right hand at the side of the punchbag . . .
3. . . . and the same again with the left hand at the other side of the punchbag. At this point an opponent would probably drop his guard.
4. Propping yourself on the punchbag with the left hand . . .
5. . . . deliver a strike at the punchbag with the right lower arm . . .
6. . . . and bring the left arm back up . . .
7. . . . delivering a further strike with the right lower arm.

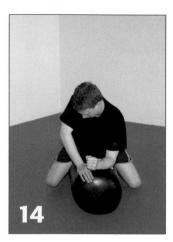

8. Bring the left hand up . . .
9. . . . and deliver a closed-hand strike with the left hand at the side of the punchbag . . .
10. . . . and the same again with the open left hand at the other side of the punchbag.
11. Place the right hand on the punchbag and bring the left lower arm up in the air . . .
12. . . . and deliver a strike at the punchbag with the left lower arm.
13. Bring the left arm back up once again . . .
14. . . . and deliver a further strike at the punchbag with the left lower arm.

1. Lie across the punchbag on the ground and stretch the right leg back up . . .

2. . . . and deliver a strike with the knee at the bag.

3. Now stretch the left leg back up . . .

4. . . . and deliver a further strike with left knee.

5. Lift the right arm up . . .

6. . . . and deliver a strike with the elbow at the bag…

7. . . . followed by lifting up the left arm . . .

8. . . . and using this arm deliver a strike with the elbow at the punchbag.

1. Sit on the punchbag on the ground and bring the right arm up rapidly.

2. Deliver a strike downwards with the elbow...

3. ...and bring the arm back up again...

4. ...to deliver a further strike downwards with the elbow.

5. Bring the left arm up rapidly...

6. ...and deliver a strike downwards with the elbow of the left arm...

7. ...and bring the left arm back up again...

8. ...and deliver a further elbow strike downwards.

1.4.7 Further Training Exercises Using the Punchbag

1. Stand with your legs two shoulder-widths apart.

2. In this position bend your knees . . .

3. . . . and stretch the legs back up again.

1. Lie down on the ground with your legs raised up and angled so that your feet are as close to your bottom as possible. The punchbag is lying across your hips held in both of your hands.

2. Now lift up your hips . . .

3. . . . and let them drop down again onto the ground.

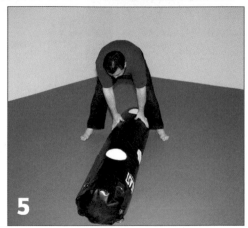

1. Pick up the punchbag from where it is lying on the ground . . .

2. . . . and having placed it on your right shoulder . . .

3. . . . throw it back down onto the ground.

4. Pick it up again. Lift it up onto your left shoulder . . .

5. . . . and throw it down again onto the ground.

1. Hold the punchbag firmly between the legs sitting on the ground (guard position).

2.-5. In this position carry out repeated strikes at it using the fists and the elbows.

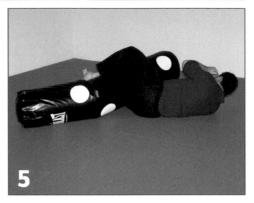

1. Hold the punchbag firmly between the legs lying on the ground (guard position).

2. Swing the punchbag over to the left-hand side . . .

3. . . . and in this position deliver several punches at the bag . . .

4. . . . then bring it back up to the start position . . .

5. . . . and swing the bag down to the right-hand side where you deliver several punches again there.

1.5   Punching and Kicking Techniques to Music

Nowadays, there are several types of sport that use music to accompany the shadow boxing and kicking drills. The music is in four-four time. It is advisable to always count to eight beats while doing either four or eight (dependent on speed) of the techniques. One can always leave out a beat to count as a pause.

Use half speed while carrying out the exercises for the first time, for example, you count to eight but only carry out four technique actions. Once you are used to it you can carry on with all eight movements.

Exercise 1:

1.   Stand with your left leg forward . . .

2.   . . . and do a jabbing punch with the left hand at head height.

Exercise 2:

1. Stand with your left leg forward . . .

2. . . . and cross punch with the right hand at head height. When delivering the punch, the shoulder is first pushed forward, then the elbow and last the fist.

Exercise 3:

1. Stand with your left leg forward . . .

2. . . . and do a jabbing punch with the left hand at head height . . .

3. . . . then deliver a right-handed cross at head height. When delivering the punch, the shoulder is first pushed forward, then the elbow and last the fist.

Exercise 4:

1. Stand with your left leg forward . . .

2. . . . and do a jabbing punch with the left hand at head height . . .

3. . . . then deliver a right-handed cross at head height. When delivering the punch, the shoulder is first pushed forward, then the elbow and last the fist.

4. This is followed by delivering a swinging hook with the left fist at head height . . .

5. . . . and finally a cross with the right hand at head height.

Exercise 5:

1. Stand with your left leg forward . . .

2. . . . and do a jabbing punch with the left hand at head height . . .

3. . . . then deliver a right-handed cross at head height. When delivering the punch, the shoulder is first pushed forward, then the elbow and last the fist.

4. This is followed by delivering an uppercut with the left fist at head height . . .

5. . . . and finally a cross with the right hand at head height.

Exercise 6:

1. Stand with your left leg forward . . .

2. . . . and do a jabbing punch with the left hand at head height . . .

3. . . . then deliver a right-handed cross at head height. When delivering the punch, the shoulder is first pushed forward, then the elbow and last the fist.

4. This is followed by delivering a further jabbing punch with the left fist at head height . . .

5. . . . and ends with a pause beat by holding the fists on guard in front of the upper body.

Exercise 7:

1. Stand with your left leg forward . . .

2. . . . and hook punch with the left hand at head height . . .

3. . . . then deliver a right-handed hook at stomach height.

4. This is followed by delivering a further left-handed hook at head height . . .

5. . . . and ends with a pause beat by holding the fists on guard in front of the upper body.

Exercise 8:

1. Stand with your left leg forward . . .

2. . . . and do a jabbing punch with the left hand at head height . . .

3. . . . then deliver a right-handed cross at head height. When delivering the punch, the shoulder is first pushed forward, then the elbow and last the fist.

4. This is followed by delivering an uppercut with the left fist . . .

5. . . . and finally a strike forwards with the elbow of the right arm. The left arm ends up above and parallel to the right arm to protect the head.

Exercise 9:

1. Stand with your left leg forward . . .

2. . . . and lift the right knee up . . .

3. . . . pushing the hips forward and performing a kick.

Exercise 10:

1. Stand with your left leg forward . . .

2. . . . and do a jabbing punch with the left hand at head height . . .

3. . . . then deliver a right-handed cross at head height. When delivering the punch, the shoulder is first pushed forward then the elbow and last the fist.

4. This is followed by delivering an uppercut with the left fist . . .

5. . . . and finally a kick forwards with the right leg. Firstly, the right leg is lifted up, the hips are pushed forwards and then comes the kick.

Exercise 11:

1. Stand with your left leg forward . . .

2. . . . and lift the right knee up . . .

3. . . . turn the hips inwards and push them forwards performing a semi-circular roundhouse style kick. The target height (head or upper body) can be varied to suit your flexibility and agility.

Exercise 12:

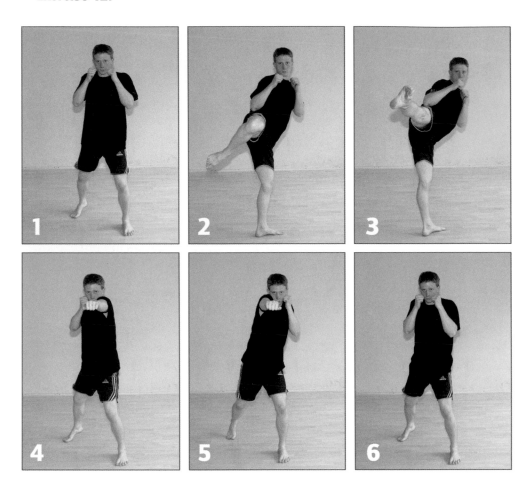

1. Stand with your left leg forward . . .

2. . . . and lift up the right leg at an angle . . .

3. . . . and perform a semi-circular kick with the right leg at head or upper body height.

4. . . . This is followed by doing a jabbing punch with the left hand . . .

5. . . . and then a right-handed cross . . .

6. . . . and finally the arms and fists adopt a guard position as a pause beat.

Exercise 13:

1. Stand with your left leg forward . . .

2. . . . and lift the right knee up to the chest . . .

3. . . . pushing the hips forward and performing a sideways kick. The target height (head or upper body) can be varied to suit your flexibility and agility.

1.6   Strengthening Exercises

At the beginning, repeat each of the selected exercises 10-15 times in 3 sets with a pause of about one minute between the sets. As soon as you can do all the exercises without a problem, you can increase the number of exercises you do.

1.6.1   Exercises for the Chest, Arm and Shoulder Muscles

1. Stand upright as normal. Stretch both arms out in front of you with the palms facing upwards.
2. Close the hands up into fists . . .
3. . . . and now open them again.

1. Stand upright as normal. Stretch both arms up above your head with the palms facing forwards.
2. Close the hands up into fists . . .
3. . . . and now open them again.

Push-up

For beginners
Step 1:

1. Get down on your hands and knees. Place both your hands close together on the ground so that the thumbs are touching each other.

2. Bend your upper arms and bring your nose down towards the ground.

3. Stretch your arms and push back up again.

Step 2:

1. Get down on your hands and knees. Push your hips forward so that your hip joints are at 180°. Place both your hands close together on the ground so that the thumbs are touching each other.

2. Bend your upper arms and bring your nose down towards the ground.

3. Stretch your arms and push back up again.

For Advanced Students:

1. Get down in the push-up position. The body is supported up from the ground only by the hands and the balls of the feet. Your bottom must not be arched up. Push your hips forward so that your hip joints are at 180°. Place both your hands close together on the ground so that the thumbs are touching each other. The legs are placed shoulder-width apart.

2. Bend your upper arms and bring your nose down towards the ground.

3. Stretch your arms and push back up again.

1. Get down in the push-up position. The body is supported up from the ground only by the hands and the balls of the feet. Your bottom must not be arched up. Push your hips forward so that your hip joints are at 180°. Place both your hands close together on the ground so that the thumbs are touching each other. The legs are placed shoulder-width apart.

2. Bend your upper arms and bring your nose down towards the ground until your chest is touching the ground.

3. Stretch your arms and push back up again.

1. Get down in the push-up position. The body is supported up from the ground only by the hands and the balls of the feet. This time your bottom is arched up. The hands are placed on the ground underneath the shoulders.

2. Push your body forward so that your nose almost touches the ground.

3. Arch your back.

4. Push your upper body back down until the nose almost touches the ground . . .

5. . . . and return to the starting position.

This exercise above is also called *'Dands'*

1. Lie on the left-hand side of your body. Propping yourself up on the left arm, bend your legs back at an angle of about 90°.

2. Bring your right hand underneath your right thigh . . .

3. . . . and pull your right thigh up to your chest.

4. Bring your right thigh back down slowly into the starting position.

Repeat this exercise 10-15 times and then do it on the other side of the body.

1. Sit down on the ground. Place your right leg back up with your left leg staying stretched out. Place the right arm on the underside of the right thigh with the right hand grasping the right leg by the hollow at the back of the knee.

2. Angle your right arm and pull your right thigh up towards your chest.

3. Stretch your right thigh back down against the pressure of your right hand.

Repeat this exercise 10-15 times and then do it with the other arm and leg.

91

1.6.2   Exercises for the Stomach

Take care when doing these exercises that the lower back is firmly on the ground and that the back is not hollowed.

1. Lie down on your back and place the feet firmly on the ground as near as possible to your bottom.

2. Lift your upper body and stretch the arms out, bringing them over the knees.

3. Drop your upper body slowly back down again without letting your back completely touch the floor.

Repeat this exercise 15-20 times in 3 sets.

1. Lie down on your back and place the feet firmly on the ground as near as possible to your bottom.

2. Lift your upper body and stretch the arms out crossing them over.

3. Drop your upper body slowly back down again without letting your back completely touch the floor.

Repeat this exercise 15-20 times in 3 sets.

1. Lie down on your back and raise the legs up to an angle of about 45° with the upper body. Bend the legs at the knees so that they form a 90° angle. Place the forefinger of both hands on your temples.

2. Lift your chest up slowly and twist the body over to the left and bring your right elbow forward to touch your left knee.

3. Let your body drop back again slowly without letting your back completely touch the floor.

4. Lift your chest up slowly and twist the body over to the right and bring your left elbow forward to touch your right knee.

5. Let your body drop back again slowly without letting your back completely touch the floor.

Repeat this exercise 15-20 times in 3 sets.

1. Lie down on your back.
2. Raise both of the legs up off the ground and bend the right knee bringing it back towards the head as far as possible...
3. ...now stretch the right leg up into the air...
4. ...then bring it down again without it touching the ground.
5. Bend your left leg bringing it back towards the head as far as possible...
6. ...now stretch the left leg up into the air...
7. ...and bring it down again without it touching the ground.

Repeat this exercise 15-20 times in 3 sets.

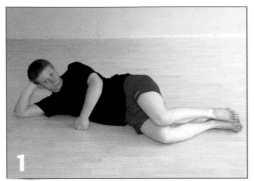

1. Lie on the right-hand side of your body. Prop yourself up with the right hand behind the head. Place your left fist down in front of your stomach.

2. Slowly lift up both of your legs that are slightly bent at the knee . . .

3. . . . and let them sink down again slowly.

Repeat this exercise 15-20 times in 3 sets, and then change sides.

1. Lie down on your back and raise both of your legs off the ground.

2. Spread your legs out wide . . .

3. Now cross your legs over each other . . .

4. . . . and spread your legs open again.

Repeat this exercise 15-20 times in 3 sets.

1. Lie down on your back and place your feet firmly on the ground as close as possible to your bottom.

2. Stretch your right leg out keeping your thighs parallel.

3. Stretch your arms out forwards and lift your upper body forwards . . .

4. . . . and then bring it back again.

Repeat this exercise 15-20 times in 3 sets.

1.6.3 Exercises for the Back

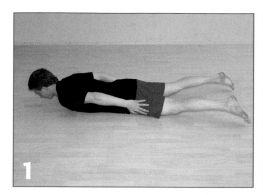 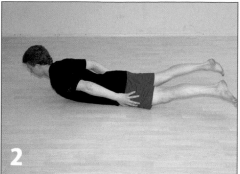

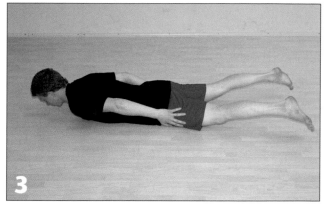

1. Lie down on your stomach with your legs spread apart and your hands by your sides.

2. Lift your upper body upwards slowly . . .

3. . . . and let it sink back down again slowly (without it touching the ground).

Repeat this exercise 15-20 times in 3 sets.

1. Lie down on your stomach with your legs spread apart. Lay your right hand on your left hand and place your forehead on your hands.

2. Lift your upper body upwards slowly . . .

3. . . . and let it sink back down again slowly (without it touching the ground).

Repeat this exercise 15-20 times in 3 sets.

1. Lie down on your stomach with your legs spread apart. Stretch both your arms forwards keeping the arms close alongside the head. Point your thumbs up at the ceiling.

2. Lift your upper body upwards slowly . . .

3. . . . and let it sink back down again slowly (without it touching the ground).

Repeat this exercise 15-20 times in 3 sets.

1. Lie down on your back and place the feet so that the heels are firmly on the ground. Tense your stomach muscles until you feel your lower back (kidneys) press against the ground.

2. Relax for a few seconds.

3. Press your bottom against the floor by tensing your back muscles. Your back should hollow a little when doing this.

Repeat this exercise 15-20 times in 3 sets.

1. Lie down on your back with your arms outstretched as support and your legs bent up at the knees.

2. From this position, lift your bottom up towards the ceiling.

3. Let your bottom drop down again slowly.

Repeat this exercise 15-20 times in 3 sets.

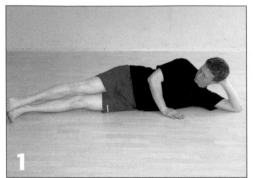

1. Lie on the left-hand side of your body. Prop yourself up with the left hand behind the head.

2. Slowly lift up both of your legs from the floor and hold them tensed up for about 5 seconds . . .

3. . . . and then let them sink down again slowly.

Repeat this exercise 15-20 times in 2-3 sets, and then change sides.

1. Get down on your hands and knees.

2. Pull your head back and up at the neck and hollow your back, tensing the back muscles.

3. Return to the starting position again.

Repeat this exercise 15-20 times in 3 sets.

1. Get down on your hands and knees.

2. Pull your chin down onto your chest and arch your back.

3. Return to the starting position again.

Repeat this exercise 15-20 times in 3 sets.

1. Get down on your hands and knees.

2. Stretch your right leg out and keep your head held horizontally.

3. Bend your right leg at the knee and bend your head under so that you can touch your head with your knee.

4. Repeat the exercise.

Repeat this exercise 15-20 times in 3 sets and then carry it out with the left leg.

1.6.4 Exercises for the Thighs

1. Lie down on your back. Bend your legs at the knees and anchor your left foot firmly on the floor.

2. Stretch the right leg right up into the air until your back starts to lift off the floor.

3. Let your right leg down again – stretched out and not quite touching the floor.

Repeat this exercise 20-30 times in 2-3 sets; then do again with the other leg.

1. Get down on your hands and knees.

2. Stretch your right leg out so that it stays in line with your back. Keep your head held straight with eyes looking at the floor.

3. Bend your right leg up at the knee . . .

4. . . . and stretch it out again.

Repeat this exercise 20-30 times in 2-3 sets; then do again with the other leg.

1. Get down on your hands and knees.

2. Lift up your right leg and bend it up at the knee. Keep your head held straight with eyes looking at the floor. Bring your right leg up under the body . . .

3. . . . and stretch it out again.

Repeat this exercise 20-30 times in 2-3 sets; then do again with the other leg.

1. Get down on your hands and knees.

2. Stretch your right leg out so that it stays in line with your back. Keep your head held straight with eyes looking at the floor. Bring your right leg up sideways at the knee . . .

3. . . . and back down again.

Repeat this exercise 20-30 times in 2-3 sets; then do again with the other leg.

1. Get down on your hands and knees.

2. Stretch your right leg out and then bring it through up to the chest . . .

3. . . . and kick backwards with the leg by straightening it.

4. Bring your right leg back into the starting position again.

Repeat this exercise 20-30 times in 2-3 sets; then do again with the other leg.

1. Lie down on the left side of your body. Prop yourself up on your left elbow.

2. Lift up your right leg bent at the knee and from this position perform a semi-circular roundhouse kick forwards by stretching the leg forwards.

3. Bring the leg back into the starting position.

Repeat this exercise 20-30 times in 2-3 sets; then do again with the other leg.

1.   Stand upright as normal.

2.   With the right leg take a lunge step forwards. Keep your back straight.

3.   Bend your right knee so that your left knee almost touches the floor.

4.   Stretch your right leg back up but not quite fully.

Make sure this exercise is done fluidly. Repeat 20-30 times; then do again with the other leg.

1. Stand upright as normal.

2. Bend both knees until the thighs are at right angles to the lower leg.

3. Stretch your legs back up but not quite fully.

Repeat this exercise 30-40 times in 3 sets.

1. Stand upright as normal.

2. Lift up onto the toes.

3. Bend your knees until the thigh are at right angles to the lower leg. Feel your heel bone with your fingers.

4. Stretch your legs back up but not quite fully.

Repeat this exercise 30-40 times in 3 sets.

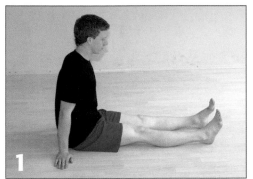

1. Sit down on the ground. Your body is at right angles to your legs. Your arms prop you up from behind.

2. Lift the outstretched right leg as far up as you can and hold this position for a short while . . .

3. . . . then let it sink back down again towards the floor but not quite touching it.

Repeat this exercise 15-20 times in 3 sets and then do it with the other leg.

1.7 Exercises Using the Medicine Ball

Most of the following exercises serve to improve the punching techniques.

1. Hold the medicine ball in the right hand . . .

2. . . . and throw it with full force against a wall 1.5-2 m away.

3. Catch it on the rebound.

After 1 minute, do the same exercise with the left hand.

1. Hold the medicine ball in both hands . . .

2. . . . and throw it against a wall 1.5-2 m away.

3. Catch it on the rebound.

1. Stand about 1.5-2 m away from a wall with your back to it. Hold the medicine ball in both hand.

2. Twist to the left towards the wall . . .

3. . . . and throw it against the wall.

Then do the same exercise on the other side. Exercise for 1-2 minutes.

1. Hold the medicine ball in both hands . . .

2. With force, stretch out both arms forwards . . .

3. . . . and pull them quickly back again.

Exercise for 1-2 minutes.

1. Hold the medicine ball in both hands . . .

2. . . . stretch both arms quickly upwards . . .

3. . . . and pull them down quickly again.

Exercise for 1-2 minutes.

1. The medicine ball is lying on the ground.

2. Deliver quick rapid punches at the medicine ball beginning with the right fist . . .

3. . . . following up with the left fist.

Exercise for 1-2 minutes.

1. Hold the medicine ball in both hands in front of the chest . . .

2. . . . and stretch both arms forwards . . .

3. . . . turn the ball over counterclockwise to the left . . .

4. . . . and then clockwise to the right.

Exercise for 1-2 minutes.

1.   Hold the medicine ball in both hands . . .

2.   . . . stretch both arms quickly upwards . . .

3.   . . . and throw the ball down on the ground with force.

Exercise for 1-2 minutes.

1. Hold the medicine ball in both hands...

2. ...and bend the body forwards at right angles to the ground, holding the medicine ball against the chest.

3. Stretch the arms with the ball downwards and drop the ball with force onto the ground.

Exercise for 1-2 minutes.

1. Sit on the ground with the legs outstretched and grab hold of the medicine ball from behind the right-hand side of the body.

2. Bring the ball around over the legs to the other side . . .

3. . . . and place it down behind the body.

Exercise for 1-2 minutes.

1. Sit on the ground with the legs outstretched and grab hold of the medicine ball from behind into your right hand.

2. Lift the right leg up and bring the ball underneath the right leg ...

3. ... take it into your left hand ...

4. ... lift the left leg ...

5. ... and bring the ball around under the left leg.

Exercise for 1-2 minutes.

1. Lie down on the ground on your back facing a wall. The knees are bent up slightly and the medicine ball lies on the stomach in both hands.

2. Lift your upper body up and throw the ball at the wall.

3. Catch it and lie back down again.

Exercise for 1-2 minutes.

1. Lie on your stomach facing a wall about 1 m away. Hold the medicine ball in both hands.

2. Lift the upper body up and throw the ball at the wall . . .

3. . . . then catch it again.

Exercise for 1-2 minutes.

1. Lie on the ground on your back holding the medicine ball in the right hand.

2. Throw the ball upwards . . .

3. . . . then catch it again.

After exercising for 1 minute do the exercise again with the left hand.

1. Lie on the ground on your back holding the medicine ball in both hands.

2. Throw the ball upwards as far as possible...

3. ...then catch it again...

4. ...and bring it above and behind the head in both hands...

5. ...and then bring it back to the starting position on the stomach.

Exercise for 1-2 minutes.

1. Lie on the ground on your back holding the medicine ball in both hands.

2. Bring the arms holding the ball behind the head, lifting the legs up at the same time . . .

3. . . . then bring the ball forwards until you can touch it with the toes of the feet.

4. Then bring the ball behind the head in both hands of the outstretched arms.

Exercise for 1-2 minutes.

1. You are in the push-up position. Both of your hands are on the medicine ball.

2. Bend the arms and let your body sink down.

3. Push-up again . . .

4. . . . and let go of the medicine ball . . .

5. . . . and as you come down again grab hold of the medicine ball again.

Exercise for 30 seconds to 1 minute.

1. You are in the push-up position. Your left hand is on the medicine ball.

2. You do a push-up . . .

3. . . . and jump over the medicine ball, placing the right hand on the medicine ball . . .

4. . . . and doing a push-up.

Exercise for 30 seconds to 1 minute.

1. You are in the push-up position. Each of your hands is on a medicine ball.

2. Do a push-up and try to get your chest as near as possible to the ground.

3. Return to the normal position.

Exercise for 30 seconds to 1 minute.

1. You are in the push-up position. Each of your feet is on a medicine ball.

2. Do a push-up and try to get your chest as near as possible to the ground.

3. Return to the normal position.

Exercise for 30 seconds to 1 minute.

1. Several medicine balls lie around the room.

2. You run off, bend the knee and touch a medicine ball with your hand . . .

3. . . . lift up again and run to the next ball . . .

4. . . . and do the same again.

5. Keep running between the balls until you reach the last one . . .

6. . . . bend down and touch this ball also. You then run backwards back to the start.

Exercise for 30 seconds to 1 minute.

1.   Hold the medicine ball in both hands . . .

2.   . . . and stretch the arms out forwards and hold the tension for 30 seconds.

3.   Return to the starting position.

Do four repeats with a 15 second pause between each.

1.   Hold the medicine ball in both hands . . .

2.   . . . and stretch the arms out forwards and lift the ball up quickly about 10 cm . . .

3.   . . . and bring it down 10 cm again.

Exercise for 1 minute. Do three repeats with a 15 second pause between each repeat.

1. Hold the medicine ball in both hands . . .

2. . . . and bring the arms with the ball back behind the head . . .

3. . . . and stretch the ball up quickly . . .

4. . . . and bring it down again.

Exercise for 1 minute. Then take a 30 second pause. Do three repeats.

1. In a sitting position, balance with one hand each on a medicine ball.

2. Now do a push-up by dropping the arms bent and bringing your bottom close to the floor. The legs remain stretched out.

3. Stretch your arms up again and press yourself up.

Exercise for 1 minute. Then take a 30 second pause. Do three repeats.

1. In a sitting position, balance with one hand each on a medicine ball. Your legs are closed and are balanced on a third medicine ball.

2. Now do a backwards push-up by dropping the bent arms and bringing your bottom close to the floor. The legs remain stretched out.

3. Stretch your arms up again and press yourself up.

Exercise for 1 minute. Then take a 30 second pause. Do three repeats.

For Advanced Students:

1. In a sitting position, balance with one hand each on a medicine ball. Both the legs are lifted up.

2. Now do a backwards push-up by dropping the bent arms and bringing your bottom close to the floor. The legs remain stretched out.

3. Stretch your arms up again and press yourself up.

Exercise for 1 minute. Then take a 30 second pause. Do three repeats.

1. Lie on the ground on your back resting the back of the head on the medicine ball.

2. Pressing down on the medicine ball with the head, lift the upper body up.

3. Drop the head and chest back down.

Exercise for 1 minute. Then take a 30 second pause. Do three repeats.

1. Stand, holding the medicine ball in the right hand . . .

2. . . . and push it upwards . . .

3. . . . and take hold of it in both hands . . .

4. . . . passing it over to the left hand . . .

5. . . . and bring it down again.

Exercise for 2 minutes. Then take a 30 second pause. Do three repeats.

1. Stand, holding a medicine ball in each hand . . .

2. . . . and push them upwards . . .

3. . . . and bring them down again.

Exercise for 1 minute. Then take a 30 second pause. Do three repeats.

1. Stand, holding a medicine ball in each hand . . .

2. . . . and push them upwards . . .

3. . . . and bring them down again behind the shoulders . . .

4. . . . and push them upwards again . . .

5. . . . bringing them in front of the shoulders . . .

Exercise for 1 minute. Then take a 30 second pause. Do three repeats.

1.8　Exercises Using the Resistance Band

You can find various resistance bands for sale in various different stiffness grades and lengths. I prefer one that is at least 3 m long. You should get some advice regarding the band stiffness from a specialist. Most specialist sports shops stock these bands and you will also find them advertised on the internet.

Tie two loops in the band and fix its center on an object about 50 cm high.

1.　Stand with your left leg forwards. Hold your head upright and lift your chest up. Place your hands in the loops and spread your fingers out.

2.　With bent arms, lift your arms outwards until your thumbs are on the outside. Breathe out.

3.　Slowly bring your arms back down into the starting position.

Repeat the exercise 15 times and then change the leading foot.

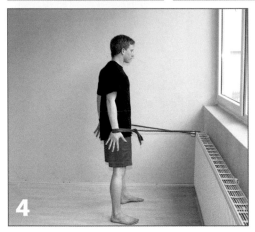

1. Stand with your left leg forwards. Hold the head upright and lift your chest up. Place your hands in the loops and spread your fingers out.

2. Lift your arms upwards . . .

3. . . . and do an outwards circular motion with both of your arms . . .

4. . . . and bring them further downwards.

5. Bring your arms back down into the starting position.

Repeat the exercise 15 times and then change the leading foot.

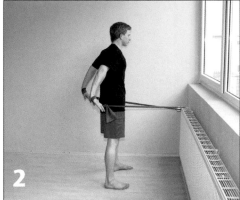

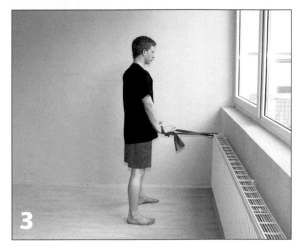

1. Stand with your left leg forwards. Hold the head upright and lift your chest up. Place your hands in the loops and spread your fingers out. Bend your wrists up so that your fingers are pointing forwards.

2. Bring your outstretched arms to the rear...

3. ...and bring your arms back into the starting position.

Repeat the exercise 15 times and then change the leading foot.

Tie two loops in the band and fix its center on an object about 50 cm high.

1. Stand at right angles to the band. Hold one end of the band firmly in your left hand and place your right hand in the loop.

2. Pull your right arm out to the right until your thumb is pointing outwards.

3. Bring your right arm back into the starting position.

Repeat the exercise 15 times and then change sides and position.

Tie two loops in the band and fix its center on an object about 50 cm high.

1. Place your right foot in one of the loops.

2. Bring your slightly bent leg backwards.

3. Bring your leg slowly back into the starting position.

Repeat the exercise 15 times and then change legs.

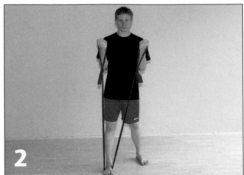

1. Tie two loops in the band and place your hands in the loops. Spread your fingers out. Place your foot down on the center of the band pinning it to the floor.

2. Lift the band up by bending up your arms by the side of your body.

3. Bring your arms back down into the starting position.

Repeat the exercise 10 times and then change leading leg.

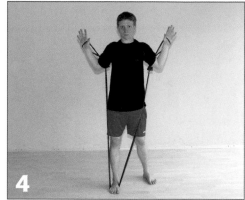

1. Tie two loops in the band and place your hands in the loops. Spread your fingers out. Place your foot down on the center of the band, pinning it to the floor.

2. Lift the band up by bending up your arms sideways . . .

3. . . . and stretching your arms upwards.

4. Bring your bent arms down sideways behind your back.

Repeat the exercise 10 times and then change leg.

1. Tie two loops in the band and place your hands in the loops and hold onto the band with both of your hands. Place both of your feet apart on the band around the center of it pinning it to the floor. Bend the body slightly forwards and push your chest out, hollowing your back a little.

2. Lift the band upwards with slightly bent arms.

3. Bring your arms back into the starting position.

Repeat the exercise 20 times.

1. Tie two loops in the band and place your hands in the loops and hold onto the band with both of your hands. Place both of your feet apart on the band around the center of it pinning it to the floor. Bend the body slightly forwards and push your chest out, hollowing your back a little.

2. Lift the band upwards and sideways with slightly bent arms.

3. Bring your arms back into the starting position.

Repeat the exercise 20 times.

1. Bend both of your arms up at the elbows so that the lower arms are at right angles to the upper arms. When doing the exercise keep the upper arms close to the body. Take hold of the band in both hands.

2. Stretch your arms, slightly bent, out to the sides with the thumbs pointing outwards.

3. Slowly bring your arms back into the starting position.

Repeat the exercise 20 times.

1. Lie down on your back and wrap the band once around each of your feet. Pull your knees up and back and take hold of the band in both hands.

2. Stretch the right leg upwards . . .

3. . . . and bring it back down again.

Repeat the exercise 20 times and then change legs.

Place the resistance band around your shoulders holding it in your left hand down by your hip. Tie a loop in the other end.

1. Take hold of the loop in your right hand. Place your left leg forwards. Beginning from the right leg, bring the hip . . .

2. . . . then the right shoulder, right elbow and right hand forwards.

3. Bring the right arm slowly back into the starting position.

Repeat the exercise 15 times and then change sides.

1. Adopt a push-up position face down. The center of the resistance band is placed over the back of the neck with your hands holding the band. Your body is touching the floor.

2. From this position, push up slowly against the band's resistance

3. . . . and let your body down again slowly.

Repeat the exercise 15 times.

Fix the band to an object around about the height of your ankle. Stand with the band behind you. Tie a loop in the end of the band. Put your left foot through the loop and place the right foot forward.

1. Put your left foot through the loop. Place the right leg forward and the left leg to the rear...

2. ...and pull the leg up bending at the knee...

3. ...then, using the hip carry out a kick forwards.

4. Bring the leg back into the bent position and lower it down into the starting position again.

Repeat the exercise 10 times and then change sides.

1.9 Specific Movement Forms/Drills

1.9.1 Lying on the Ground

Spider:

1. You are on all fours with your knees almost touching the floor. In this position move around on the floor like a spider.

2. Turn over by pushing the right leg through under the other leg ...

3. ... and then turn over.

4. To turn back pull the left leg ...

5. ... under the other one ...

6. ... turning so that you are back on all fours.

Crab/Caterpillar:

1. You are lying on your back with your knees pulled back . . .

2. . . . and push your bottom out to the left side right angles. At the same time move your arms as if you were, for example, trying to push an opponent's knees away.

3. Return to the starting position.

4. Push your bottom out to the right side at right angles. At the same time move your arms as if you were, for example, trying to push an opponent's knees away . . .

5. . . . and then return to the starting position again.

Bridge:

1. You are lying on your back with your knees pulled back up under your bottom . . .

2. . . . and push your hips up . . .

3. . . . and turn onto your left shoulder and touch the floor with your right hand.

4. Return into the starting position . . .

5. . . . and push your hips up . . .

6. . . . and turn onto your right shoulder and touch the floor with your left hand.

7. Return into the starting position.

Changeover from Bridge to Spider:

1. You are lying on your back with your knees pulled back up under your bottom . . .

2. . . . and push your hips up . . .

3. . . . and turn onto your left shoulder and touch the floor with your right hand. Keep on turning further until you are in the 'Spider' position.

4. Bring your right leg through under your left leg . . .

5. . . . and turn over to lie on your back . . .

6. . . . and let your upper body back down onto the floor.

1.9.2   Standing (Shadow Boxing)

Each sequence should last 2 minutes. Pauses between drills can be 1 minute long. You should do 10 combinations.

Breathe out through the nose and take care to always keep your cover up. Move around the room and imagine that you have an opponent in front of you.

Training Tip: Record the commands onto a CD or tape and play them when you exercise. Carry out punches and kicks as per the instructions as you listen to them.

1. Stand with your left leg forward and keep your cover up.
2. Jab with the left hand . . .
3. . . . now a right-handed cross . . .
4. . . . and a left-handed hook at liver height . . .
5. . . . now a left-handed hook at head height.
6. Do a right-handed cross . . .
7. . . . and end with a semi-circular kick at the ribs with the right leg.

1. Stand with your left leg forward and keep your cover up.

2. Do a hook with the left hand at head height...

3. ...followed by a right-handed cross.

4. Bring the right hand out to the right as if you were pushing the opponent's head to the side...

5. ...and follow this up with a left-handed hook at head height...

6. ...then a right-handed uppercut at head height.

7. ...and end with a jab at head height with the left hand.

1. Stand with your left leg forward and keep your cover up.

2. Bring your left hand forward as if to disrupt the opponent's vision.

3. This is followed by a strike with the right elbow at head height . . .

4. . . . and a hook with the left hand at head height . . .

5. . . . and now with a right-handed cross at head height.

6. Bring both hands forward together at head height as if you wanted to grab hold of the opponent by the back of the neck . . .

7. . . . and carry out a knee-up kick with the left leg at stomach height.

1. Stand with your left leg forward and keep your cover up.
2. Deliver a left-handed uppercut at liver height...
3. ...and then a cross at head height...
4. ...and now with a left-handed hook at head height.
5. Bring your left hand forward as if to disrupt the opponent's vision...
6. ...followed by a strike with the right elbow at head height...
7. Bring the left arm outwards as if you wanted to push the opponent's head to the right...
8. ...and end the combination with a left-handed jab at head height.

1. Stand with your left leg forward and keep your cover up.

2. Deliver a left-handed jab at head height...

3. ...followed by a right-handed hook at rib height.

4. Now deliver a left-handed uppercut at chin height...

5. ...and a right-handed cross at head height.

6. Bring the right arm forwards as if you wanted to grab hold of the opponent's right shoulder...

7. ...and carry out a knee-up kick with the right leg at stomach or thigh height.

1. Stand with your left leg forward and keep your cover up.
2. Deliver a left-handed hook at rib height . . .
3. . . . followed up by a left-handed hook at head height.
4. . . . and now deliver a right-handed uppercut at chin height . . .
5. . . . and a left-handed jab at head height.
6. Imagine the opponent is doing a hook with his right hand and you duck away from it . . .
7. . . . and deliver a right-handed hook at the liver . . .
8. . . . now, duck away again...
9. . . . and then carry out a left-handed hook at head height.

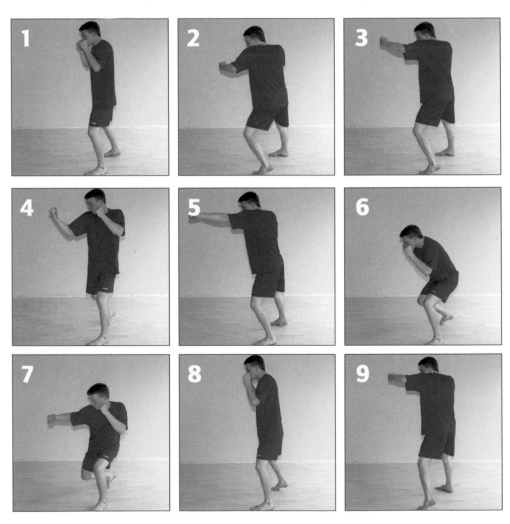

1. Stand with your left leg forward and keep your cover up.

2. Deliver a right-handed cross . . .

3. . . . followed up by a left-handed uppercut at liver height . . .

4. . . . and now deliver a right-handed overhook at head height . . .

5. . . . and a left-handed hook at liver height . . .

6. . . . and then deliver a right handed cross at head height.

7. Imagine the opponent is going to deliver a punch at your head and sweeps this with the left hand inwards. As you do this, bring your head forward and to the outside (45°).

8. Following the feint you deliver a right-handed cross at stomach height.

1.9.3 Standing (Street Fighting Drill)

1. Dance about on the spot and hold your cover well up. Now do the shadow boxing exercise (see Chapter 1.9.2.).

2. On a given command, sprint forwards about 3 m and practice giving a series of chain punches one after the other beginning with the right hand . . .

3. . . . and then a punch with the left hand . . .

4. . . . and a punch with the right hand.

5. Bring both arms and hands upwards and imagine that you are bringing your fingers behind the opponent's ears.

6. Place the thumbs in the eye sockets of an imaginary opponent and wipe them over the eyes.

7.   Place both hands behind the neck...

8.   ...and do a head butt...

9.   followed by a knee-up kick at the genitals...

10.-11. ...and finally a strike with the right elbow at the imaginary opponent's head height.

Then, start all over again from Point 1.

1.9.4 Standing (Drill to Improve Punching Strength)

The following exercises are done for 1 minute followed by a 30 second pause. Movements are carried out at full speed.

The intensity of the exercises can be increased by doing them holding light dumbbells (1-2 kg).

1.-3. Do a series of rapid chain punches moving forwards.

1. Stretch the arms upwards . . .

2. . . . and bend the arms back so that the hands come behind the head . . .

3. . . . and now stretch the arms up again.

1. Stretch the arms forward. The fists are clenched and held in the vertical position.

2. Move the outstretched arms up and down . . .

3. . . . the fists should only be about one fist difference in the amount of movement in the up and down actions.

1. Stretch the arms out to the side. The palms of the hands are pointing at the floor.

2. Bring the outstretched arms up sideways . . .

3. . . . and back down again.

1. Stretch the arms out to the side. The clenched fists are held horizontally.

2. Bring the outstretched arms up sideways . . .

3. . . . and back down again.

1. Bend the body forwards at right angles and let the arms hang downwards.

2. From this position fling the arms outstretched to the sides . . .

3. . . . and back down again.

1. Bend your arms up close to each side of the body...

2. ...and do a rapid uppercut punching movement with the left fist...

3. ...and then one with the right fist.

1. Crouch on one knee and hold the position . . .

2. . . . while doing a rapid punching movement forwards with the left hand . . .

3. . . . and then followed by the right hand.

1.10   Circuit Training Exercises at Stations

In Circuit Training – a special form of fitness training – exercises are done at various stations that are visited one after the other. At each station, a certain exercise has to be performed. So – for example – exercises to improve stamina, speed, agility and strength can be concentrated on – each at one station. The stations are best positioned in a circle inside a room.

As a general rule, as you move from one station to the next, the exercises will cover the different muscle groups.

You can put your own training circuit together by choosing exercises from those covered in previous chapters. They can be solo exercises and even exercises with a partner. You can also alternate between the strengthening exercises and stretching exercises that are covered in the next chapter of this book.

Exercises should be done for 2 minutes at each station. After completing the exercise at the one station, you then move on to the next station. Pauses of between 30 seconds and 1 minute should be taken between each exercise.

Station # 1
Material required: Skipping rope

Do skipping on the spot.

Station # 2
Material required: Medicine ball

1. Hold the medicine ball in the right hand ...

2. ... and throw it with full force against a wall 2-3 m away.

3. Catch the ball as it comes back.

After 1 minutes' exercise do the same exercise with the left hand.

Station # 3

1. Get down in the push-up position. The body is supported up from the ground only by the hands and the balls of the feet. This time your bottom is arched up. The hands are placed on the ground underneath the shoulders.

2. Push your body forward so that your nose almost touches the ground.

3. Arch your back.

4. Push your upper body back down until the nose almost touches the ground (this exercise is also called 'Dands')...

5. ... and return to the starting position.

Station # 4

1. Get down on your hands and knees.

2. Pull your head back and up at the neck and hollow your back, tensing the back muscles.

3. Return to the starting position again.

4. Pull your chin down onto your chest and arch your back.

5. Return to the starting position again.

Station # 5
Material required: Medicine ball

1. Hold the medicine ball in both hands and bring it back behind your head . . .

2. . . . and throw the ball at a wall 2-3 m away.

3. Catch the ball as it rebounds.

Station # 6

1. Stand normally.

2. Take a large lunge step forwards with the right leg. Hold your back straight.

3. Bend your right knee until the knee almost touches the floor.

4. Now stretch back up onto your right leg.

Station # 7

1. Lie down on your back and raise the legs up to an angle of about 45° with the upper body. Bend the legs at the knees so that they form 90°. Place the forefinger of both hands on your temples.

2. Lift your chest up slowly and twist the body over to the left and bring your right elbow forward to touch your left knee.

3. Let your body drop back again slowly without letting your back completely touch the floor.

4. Lift your chest up slowly and twist the body over to the right and bring your left elbow forward to touch your right knee.

5. Let your body drop back again slowly without letting your back completely touch the floor.

Station # 8
Material required: Medicine ball

1. You are in the push-up position. Your left hand is on the medicine ball.

2. You do a push-up . . .

3. . . . and jump over the medicine ball, placing the right hand on the medicine ball . . .

4. . . . and do a push-up.

Station # 9
1.-3. Do a Jumping Jack

Station # 10
Material required: Punchbag

1. Hold the punchbag firmly between the legs sitting on the ground (guard position).

2.-5. In this position carry out repeated strikes at it using the fists and the elbows.

Station # 11
Material required: Punchbag

1. Stand with your legs two shoulder-widths apart.

2. In this position bend your knees . . .

3. . . . and stretch the legs back up again.

Station # 12
Material required: Medicine ball

1. Lie on the ground on your back holding the medicine ball in the right hand.

2. Throw the ball upwards . . .

3. . . . then catch it again.

After exercising for 1 minute do the exercise again with the left hand.

Station # 13

1. Lie down on your stomach with your legs spread apart. Lay your right hand on your left hand and place your forehead on your hands.

2. Lift your upper body upwards slowly...

3. ...and let it sink back down again slowly (without it touching the ground).

Station # 14

1. Get down on your hands and knees.

2. Stretch your right leg out so that it stays in line with your back. Keep your head held straight with eyes looking at the floor.

3. Bend your right leg up at the knee . . .

4. . . . and stretch it out again.

Station # 15
Material required: Punchbag

1.-2. Standing in front of the punchbag, carry out rapid short jabbing hits for 10 seconds, with at the same time rapid steps on the spot.

3.-5. Drop down into the push-up position and do a push-up.

2 Partner and Group Training

2.1 Training with Punch Mitts

Starting position for the wearer of the punch mitts:

The partner – B – wearing the punch mitts, stands in front of A and is holding both of the mitts at stomach height. A and B move around the room. As soon as B has placed the mitts into the starting position, A can start punching at B with his combinations. A must take care that he pulls his fists back quickly and keeps his head covered at all times. B uses the punch mitt to throw punches back towards A's head. This will indicate if A has moved back quickly enough and whether he is covering his head with the arms sufficiently enough.

Rounds last 2 minutes followed by a pause of 1 minute. Do a total of at least 10 rounds.

1. A and B stand opposite each other. B is holding both mitts up at stomach height.

2. A delivers a quick uppercut with his left fist . . .

3. . . . and then a right-handed one at the mitt.

1. A and B stand opposite each other. B is holding both mitts up at head height.

2. A delivers quick jab punches with his left fist . . .

3. . . . and his right fist at the mitts.

1. A and B stand opposite each other. B is holding both mitts up at stomach height.

2. A delivers a quick uppercut with his right fist . . .

3. . . . and then a left-handed one at the mitts.

4. After a minute's practice, B changes the position of the mitts to head height and A delivers quick jab punches with his right fist . . .

5. . . . and his left fist at the mitts.

1. A and B stand opposite each other with their left legs leading.

2. B lifts his right mitt up to head height. A takes a gliding step with the left leading leg forwards towards B and at the same time delivers a jab punch with his left fist at the right mitt.

3. A delivers a cross at the mitt with his right fist . . .

4. . . . and then takes a gliding step backwards with his rear leg.

1. A and B stand opposite each other with their left legs leading.

2. B lifts his left mitt up to head height. A takes a gliding step with the left leading leg forwards towards B and at the same time delivers a jab punch with his left fist at the left mitt . . .

3. . . . and then takes a gliding step backwards with his rear leg.

203

1. A and B stand opposite each other with their left legs leading.

2. B lifts both mitts up to head height. A takes a gliding step with the left leading leg forwards towards B and at the same time delivers a jab punch with his left fist at the left mitt . . .

3. . . . followed by a cross with the right fist at the right mitt . . .

4. . . . ending with a left-handed jabbing punch at the left mitt.

5. A then takes a gliding step backwards with his rear leg.

1. A and B stand opposite each other with their left legs leading.

2. B lifts both mitts up to head height. The left mitt is at right angles to the right mitt. A takes a gliding step with the left leading leg forwards towards B and at the same time delivers a jab punch with his left fist at the right mitt.

3. A delivers a cross with the right fist at the right mitt . . .

4. . . . a hook with the left fist at the left mitt . . .

5. . . . and a further cross with the right fist at the right mitt.

6. A then takes a gliding step backwards with his rear leg.

1. A and B stand opposite each other with their left legs leading.

2. B lifts both mitts up to head height. The left mitt is at right angles to the right mitt. A takes a gliding step with the left leading leg forwards towards B and at the same time delivers a jab punch with his left fist at the right mitt.

3. A delivers a cross with the right fist at the right mitt . . .

4. . . . an uppercut with the left fist at the left mitt . . .

5. . . . and a further cross with the right fist at the right mitt.

6. A then takes a gliding step backwards with his rear leg.

1. A and B stand opposite each other with their left legs leading.

2. B places the right mitt onto the side of his upper body at hip height and the left mitt is lifted up to his right shoulder. A takes a gliding step with the left leading leg forwards towards B and pulls his left arm back.

3. A delivers a hook with his left fist at the right mitt . . .

4. . . . and pulls his left arm back . . .

5. . . . and delivers a further hook at the left mitt.

6. A then takes a gliding step backwards with his rear leg.

1. A and B stand opposite each other. A leads with his left leg.

2. B takes a gliding step forwards with the right leg and holds the right mitt pointing horizontally forwards at hip height. A delivers an uppercut with his right fist at the right mitt and then at the same time takes a gliding step backwards.

3. B takes a gliding step forwards with the right leg and holds the right mitt pointing horizontally forwards at hip height. A delivers an uppercut with his left fist at the left mitt and then at the same time takes a gliding step backwards.

4. B takes a gliding step forwards with the right leg and holds the right mitt pointing horizontally forwards at hip height. A delivers an uppercut with his right fist at the right mitt and then at the same time takes a gliding step backwards.

5. B holds the left mitt at right angles forward and A delivers a hook with his left fist at the left mitt.

6. B lifts the right mitt up to the right-hand side of his head and A delivers a cross with his right fist at the right mitt.

7. A then takes a gliding step backwards with his rear leg.

1. A and B stand opposite each other. A leads with his left leg.

2. B lifts both mitts – one over the other – up in front of his head. A takes a gliding step forwards with the left leg towards B and delivers a jab with his right fist at the front mitt.

3. A takes a step forwards with the right leg and at the same time delivers a jab with his left fist at the front mitt.

4. A takes a further step forwards with the left leg and at the same time delivers a jab with his right fist at the front mitt.

5. A does a semi-circular roundhouse kick (Mawashi geri) at B's left ribcage.

6. A then takes a gliding step with his rear leg backwards.

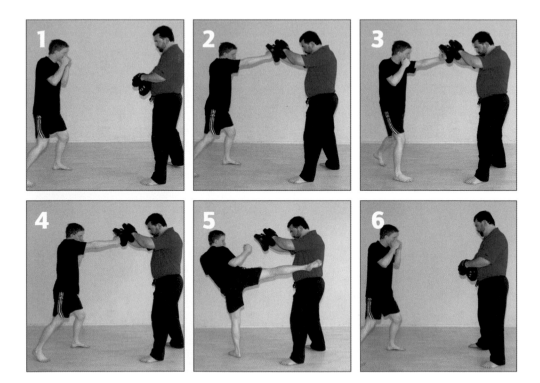

1. A and B stand opposite each other. Both lead with their left legs. B lifts both mitts – one over the other – horizontally in front of his stomach. A takes a gliding step forwards with the forward leg towards B and places his left hand on B's left shoulder and the right hand on top of the mitts . . .

2. . . . and then puts his left leg to the rear.

3. A delivers a knee-up kick at the mitts.

4. A then takes a gliding step with his rear leg backwards.

1. A and B stand opposite each other. Both lead with their left legs.

2. B is standing at right angles to A. B is holding both mitts on his backside.

3. A takes a step to the left sideways with the left leg . . .

4. . . . and delivers a roundhouse kick with his right foot at the mitts.

5. A then takes a gliding step with his rear leg backwards.

1. A and B stand opposite each other. Both lead with their left legs.

2. B is holding the right mitt in front of the inside of his right thigh. A takes a step to the left sideways with the left leg . . .

3. . . . and delivers a lowkick with his right foot at the right mitt.

4. A then takes a gliding step with his rear leg backwards.

1. A and B stand opposite each other. Both lead with their left legs.

2. B is holding the left mitt in front of the outside of his left thigh.

3. A delivers a lowkick with his right foot at the left mitt.

4. A then takes a gliding step with his rear leg backwards.

1. A and B stand opposite each other. Both lead with their left legs.

2. B is holding the left mitt on the left side of his body. A takes a step to the right with the right leg and lifts his right leg up . . .

3. . . . and delivers a kick with his right foot sideways at the left mitt.

4. A then takes a gliding step with his rear leg backwards.

1. A and B stand opposite each other. Both lead with their left legs.

2. B twists to the left and holds both mitts up at the left side of his body. A takes a step to the right with the right leg . . .

3. . . . and delivers a roundhouse kick (Mawashi geri) with his right foot forwards at the mitts.

4. A then takes a gliding step with his rear leg backwards.

1. A and B stand opposite each other. Both lead with their left legs.

2. B holds the right mitt up to head height. A takes a gliding step forwards with his left leg and lifts his right arm up and bends it . . .

3. . . . and delivers a strike with his elbow at the mitt.

4. A then takes a gliding step with his rear leg backwards.

1. A and B stand opposite each other. Both lead with their left legs.

2. B holds the right mitt up to head height. A takes a gliding step forwards with his left leg and lifts his right arm up and bends it . . .

3. . . . and delivers an upwards strike with his elbow at the mitt.

4. A then takes a gliding step with his rear leg backwards.

1. A and B stand opposite each other. Both lead with their left legs.

2. B holds the right mitt up to head height. A takes a gliding step forward to the right with his left leg and lifts his right arm up and bends it . . .

3. . . . turning his body in a clockwise direction . . .

4. . . . and delivers a strike backwards with his elbow at the mitt.

5. A turns back again . . .

6. . . . and then takes a gliding step with his rear leg backwards.

1. A and B stand opposite each other. Both lead with their left legs.

2. B holds the right mitt up to head height. A takes a gliding step forwards with his left leg and delivers a left-handed jab.

3. A delivers a right-handed cross.

4. B lifts the left mitt up at right angles in front of the right mitt and A delivers a hook with the left fist at the left mitt.

5. B delivers a strike from outside with the right arm at A's head. A blocks this by doing a shoulder stopping movement with the left hand at B's right shoulder.

6. B holds the right mitt up to head height and A delivers a right-handed cross at the right mitt.

7. B lifts the left mitt up at right angles and A delivers a hook with the left fist at the left mitt.

8. B lifts the right mitt up to head height and A delivers a cross with the right fist at the mitt.

9. A then takes a gliding step with his rear leg backwards.

1. A and B stand opposite each other. Both lead with their left legs.

2. B holds the right mitt up to head height. A takes a gliding step forwards with his left leg and delivers a left-handed jab.

3. A delivers a right-handed cross.

4. B lifts the left mitt up at right angles in front of the right mitt and A delivers a hook with the left fist at the left mitt.

5. B delivers a strike from outside with the right arm at A's head. A executes a cover block with his left arm.

6. B holds the right mitt up to head height. A delivers a right-handed cross at the right mitt.

7. B lifts the left mitt up at right angles and A delivers a hook with the left fist at the left mitt.

8. B lifts the right mitt up to head height and A delivers a cross with the right fist at the mitt.

9. A then takes a gliding step with his rear leg backwards.

1. A and B stand opposite each other. Both lead with their left legs.

2. B holds the right mitt up to head height. A takes a gliding step forwards with his left leg and delivers a left-handed jab.

3. A delivers a right-handed cross.

4. B lifts the left mitt up at right angles and A delivers a hook with the left fist at the left mitt.

5. B delivers a strike from outside with the right arm at A's head. A dodges first to the right . . .

6. ...ducks under the striking arm and at the same time delivers a hook at B's liver.

7. B lifts the left mitt up at right angles and A delivers a hook with the left fist at the left mitt.

8. B lifts the right mitt up to head height and A delivers a cross with the right fist at the mitt.

9. A then takes a gliding step with his rear leg backwards.

1. A and B stand opposite each other. Both lead with their left legs.

2. B holds the right mitt up to head height. A takes a gliding step forwards with his left leg and delivers a left-handed jab . . .

3. and then a right-handed cross.

4. B lifts the left mitt up at right angles in front of the right mitt and A delivers a hook with the left fist at the left mitt.

5. A takes a step out to the left with his left leg . . .

6. . . . and executes a roundhouse kick (Mawashi geri) with his right leg at B's left-hand side of the ribcage.

7. A then takes a gliding step with his rear leg backwards.

1. A and B stand opposite each other. Both lead with their left legs.
2. B delivers a punch with the right hand (mitt) at A's head. A takes a gliding step forwards with his right leg, does a sweeping movement with his right hand and delivers a left-handed uppercut at B's left mitt.
3. B pulls his right hand back and holds the right mitt at head height next to the right-hand side of his head. A delivers a right-handed cross.
4. B lifts the left mitt up at right angles in front of the right mitt and A delivers a hook with the left fist at the left mitt.
5. A delivers a further cross with his right hand at the right mitt.
6. B places the left mitt on the inside of his left thigh. A takes a step out to the right with his right leg . . .
7. . . . and delivers a lowkick with his left leg at the left mitt.
8. A then takes a gliding step with his rear leg backwards.

1. A and B stand opposite each other. Both lead with their left legs.

2. B holds the right mitt at head height next to the right-hand side of his head. A takes a step forwards with his left leg and at the same time delivers a left-handed jab.

3. A delivers a further punch (cross) with his right hand at the right mitt.

4. B executes a roundhouse kick (Mawashi geri) with his right leg at A's head.

5. B pulls his right leg back, lifts the right mitt up to head height and A delivers a right-handed cross at the right mitt.

6. B lifts the left mitt up at right angles to the right mitt and A delivers a swinging punch (hook) at the left mitt.

7. B places the left mitt on the inside of his left thigh. A takes a step out to the right with his right leg . . .

8. . . . and delivers a lowkick with his left leg at the left mitt.

9. A then takes a gliding step with his rear leg backwards.

1. A and B stand opposite each other. Both lead with their left legs.

2. B holds the right mitt up at head height. A takes a gliding step forwards with his forward left leg towards B and at the same time delivers a left-handed jab at the right mitt.

3. A delivers a cross with his right hand at the right mitt.

4. B places the left mitt at right angles below the right mitt and A delivers an uppercut with his left hand at the left mitt.

5. A delivers a further punch as a right-handed cross at the right mitt.

6. B takes a lunging step to the right, preparing to deliver a lowkick with his left leg.

7. A anticipates B's move and delivers a lowkick himself at the inside of B's right thigh.

8. B lifts the right mitt up to head height and A delivers a cross with his right fist at the right mitt.

9. B lifts the left mitt up at right angles to the right mitt and A delivers a swinging punch (hook) at the left mitt.

10. B lifts the right mitt up to head height and A delivers a cross with his right fist at the right mitt.

11. A then takes a gliding step with his rear leg backwards.

1. A and B stand opposite each other. Both lead with their left legs.

2. B takes a lunging step to the left with his left leg . . .

3. . . . followed up by executing a lowkick with his right leg at the outside of A's left thigh. A anticipates this move and places his right lower arm on B's right lower leg . . .

4. . . . and carries out a counterclockwise sweeping movement down to the right with his right arm.

5. B continues to turn counterclockwise, lifting his left leg up to prevent a lowkick being executed by A.

6. B holds the right mitt up at head height and A delivers a cross with his right hand at the right mitt.

7. A then takes a gliding step with his rear leg backwards.

1.   A and B stand opposite each other. Both lead with their left legs.

2.   B holds the left mitt up in front of his stomach and A executes a forward kick.

3.   A places his right leg down forward . . .

4.   . . . and delivers a cross with his left hand at the right mitt . . .

5.   . . . and then a jab with the right hand.

6. B holds both mitts at hip height. A places his left hand on B's left shoulder protecting his chin the left upper arm . . .

7. . . . and executes a knee-up strike with the left leg at the mitts.

8. A places the left leg to the rear. B lifts the right mitt up to head height and A brings his right arm back to gain momentum . . .

9. . . . and delivers a strike with his right elbow at the right mitt.

10. A then takes a gliding step with his rear leg backwards.

1. A and B stand opposite each other. Both lead with their left legs.

2. B delivers a punch with his right hand at A's head. A sweeps the attacking arm inwards with his left hand and at the same time delivers a right-handed overhook punch over B's attacking arm at B's head.

3. B holds the left mitt on the inside of his left thigh . . .

4. . . . and A executes a lowkick with his left leg at the left mitt.

5. B holds the right mitt up at head height. A places his left leg down forwards and at the same time delivers a right-handed jab at the right mitt.

6. A then takes a gliding step with his rear leg backwards.

1. A and B stand opposite each other. Both lead with their left legs.

2. B executes a semi-circular roundhouse kick in the direction of A's left hand side ribcage. A then takes a gliding step to the right and blocks B's right leg with his left arm.

3. B holds the right mitt alongside the right hand side of his head and A delivers a right-handed cross at the mitt.

4. A then takes a gliding step with his rear leg backwards.

1.   A and B stand opposite each other. Both lead with their left legs.

2.   B executes a lowkick with his right leg in the direction of A's left thigh. A lifts his left leg sharply upwards, brings it around out to the left and executes a defensive technique with his left leg.

3.   B holds the right mitt alongside the right hand side of his head . . .

4.   . . . and A delivers a right-handed cross at the mitt.

5.   B holds the left mitt up at right angles to the right mitt and A delivers a hook with his left hand at the left mitt.

6. A delivers a further punch (cross) with his right hand at the right mitt.

7. B holds the left mitt on the inside of his left thigh . . .

8. . . . and A ends the combination by executing a lowkick with his left leg at the left mitt.

9. A then takes a gliding step with his rear leg backwards.

2.2   Strength and Stamina Training with a Partner

1.   A is standing with his legs shoulder-width apart. A is standing in front of B.

2.   A jumps up around B's hips.

3.-4.   A clambers around B's body without touching the ground.

Now change roles.

1. A is standing with his legs shoulder-width apart. A is standing behind B.

2. A jumps up onto B's back. B holds onto both of A's legs.

3. B does knee presses by dropping his body down until his knees and legs are at right angles . . .

4. . . . and then straightens his body back up again by stretching his legs.

Now change roles.

1. A and B stand with their backs to each other and arms hooked together.

2. A and B do knee bends . . .

3. . . . sit down . . .

4. . . . stretch their legs out . . .

5. . . . and pull them back in again . . .

6. . . . and press against each other to lift themselves up again . . .

7. . . . until they are standing.

Do this exercise 10-15 times.

1. A is standing in front of B.

2. A jumps up around B's hips with his arms around B's neck . . .

3. . . . and then lets his arms loose and brings his hands to his temples. A lets his body drop down . . .

4. . . . and pulls his body back up again (sit-up/crunch).

Repeat this exercise 10-15 times. Then change roles. If the partner is wearing a belt then the partner standing can get hold of it to assist with the upward pull of the body especially when this part of the exercise proves difficult.

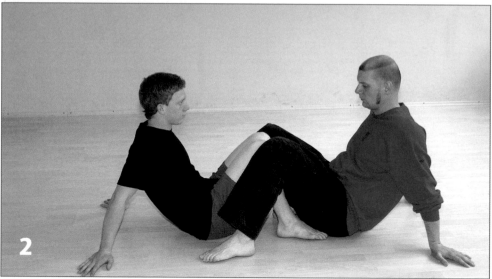

1. A and B sit down opposite each other. A's legs are on the outside and B's legs are on the inside.

2. A presses his legs inwards and B presses his legs outwards. Hold the tension for 20-30 seconds each time.

Afterwards change positions. Repeat the exercise 3 times each side.

1. A is lying on his back between B's legs. A holds his head up forwards. B is wearing a belt.

2. A gets hold of the belt around B's waist . . .

3. . . . and tenses his body out straight . . .

4. . . . and pulls himself upwards with his arms against B's body . . .

5. . . . and then lets himself fall back again slowly (without touching the ground).

Repeat the exercise 10-15 times then change.

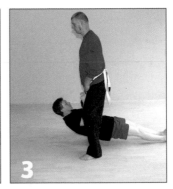

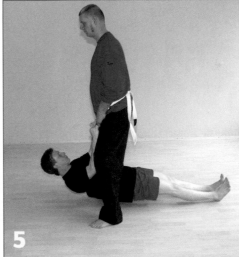

1. A is lying on his back between B's legs. A lets his head drop backwards. A is wearing a belt. B gets hold of the belt around A's waist . . .

2. . . . and pulls A's body up into a straight line . . .

3. . . . pulling A's body towards himself with his arms . . .

4. . . . and then lets A drop back again slowly (without touching the ground).

Repeat the exercise 10-15 times then change.

1. A is lying on his back between B's legs. A lets his head drop backwards.

2. B takes hold of both of A legs at the ankles and pulls A's body up into a straight line.

3. B pulls A up as far as he can to his body . . .

4. . . . and then lets A drop back again slowly (without allowing him to touch the ground totally).

Repeat the exercise 10-15 times and then change positions.

1. A is lying on his back between B's legs. A lets his head drop backwards.

2. B takes hold of the nape of A's neck and pulls A's body up into a straight line.

3. B pulls A up as far as he can to his body . . .

4. . . . and then lets A drop back again slowly (without allowing him to touch the ground totally).

Repeat the exercise 10-15 times and then change positions.

1. A is lying on his back between B's legs. A lets his head drop backwards.

2. B takes hold underneath both of A's locked-together arms . . .

3. . . . and pulls A's body up into a straight line.

4. B pulls A up as far as he can to his body . . .

5. . . . and then lets A drop back again slowly (without allowing him to touch the ground totally).

Repeat the exercise 10-15 times and then change positions.

1. A is lying on his back between B's legs. A lets his head drop backwards.

2. B takes hold of both of A's arms on the top side . . .

3. . . . and B pulls A up as far as he can to his body . . .

4. . . . and then lets A drop back again slowly (without allowing him to touch the ground totally).

Repeat the exercise 10-15 times and then change positions.

1. A is lying on his stomach in front of B. His legs are slightly spread open. B is standing between A's legs.

2. B gets hold of both legs around the ankles and lifts. A tenses his body so that his body is straight. A's hands are on the floor close to the shoulders.

3. A presses his body upwards using his arms.

4. A then lets his body slowly down again.

Repeat the exercise 10-15 times and then change positions.

1.   A is lying on his stomach in front of B. His legs are slightly spread open. B is standing between A's legs. B gets hold of both legs around the ankles and lifts. A tenses his body so that his body is straight. A's hands are on the floor close to the shoulders.

2.-3. A presses his body upwards using his arms. B now pushes A on his hands round the room like a wheelbarrow.

Repeat the exercise 10-15 times and then change positions.

1.   A is lying on his stomach in front of B. His legs are slightly spread open. B is standing between A's legs. B holds both of A's legs around the ankles and lifts. A lets his body (chest) touch the floor.

2.   A now pushes his body up sharply and claps his hands in front of him . . .

3.   . . . and lands on his hands again as he comes down.

Repeat the exercise 10-15 times and then change positions.

1. A is lying on his back between B's legs. A lets his head drop backwards. A holds onto B's ankles with both hands and lifts his legs up at right angles.

2. B takes hold of both of A's legs around the feet and pushes them away down in the direction of the floor. Take care that A doesn't arch his back as this is done. If this is the case then less impetus must be given to the pushing motion.

3. A brings his legs back up again.

4. B now pushes the legs to the left...

5. ...and A brings them back again into the central position.

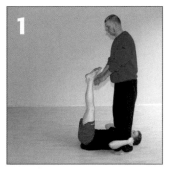

6. B now pushes them to the right...

7. ...and A brings them back again into the central position.

Repeat the exercise 10-15 times and then change positions.

1. A is standing behind B. B's arms are extended outwards to the sides and A places his hands on B's lower arms near the wrists.

2. A slowly pushes B's arms downwards while the latter tenses his arm and tries to resist the movement.

3. As soon as A manages to get B's arms pushed down . . .

4. . . . B loosens the tension on his arms a little so that . . .

5. . . . A can push B's arms back up again into the middle.

Repeat the exercise 3 times and then change positions.

1. A and B are sitting on the ground and have hooked their legs around each other's legs. Their fingers are holding their temples.

2. At the same time, A and B let their bodies fall backwards without touching the floor with their backs.

3. A and B now lift their upper bodies back up forwards without relaxing their stomach muscles.

Repeat the exercise 25-30 times and then change the leg positions.

255

1. A is on all fours on his knees to form a seat and B sits on his back and wraps his legs around A's waist. B is holding his fingers to his temples.

2. B leans backwards . . .

3. . . . and lifts his upper body back up again without relaxing his stomach muscles.

Repeat the exercise 25-30 times and then change the leg positions.

1. A is on all fours on his knees to form a seat and B sits on his back and hooks his legs forward inside A's arms. B is holding his fingers to his temples.

2. B leans backwards . . .

3. . . . and lifts his upper body back up again without relaxing his stomach muscles.

Repeat the exercise 25-30 times and then change the leg positions.

1. A is on all fours on his knees to form a seat and B sits on his back and hooks his legs forward inside A's arms. B is holding a medicine ball.

2. B leans backwards . . .

3. . . . and lifts his upper body back up again without relaxing his stomach muscles.

Repeat the exercise 25-30 times and then change the leg positions.

1. A is on all fours on his knees to form a seat and B sits on his back and hooks his legs forward inside A's arms. B is holding a medicine ball in his hands that are stretched upwards.

2. B leans backwards. The arms remain stretched out throughout this movement.

3. B then lifts his upper body back up again without relaxing his stomach muscles.

Repeat the exercise 25-30 times and then change the leg positions.

1. A stands opposite B. Both adopt a fighting position (Picture 1).
2. A takes a gliding step backwards (Picture 2).
3. B follows with a gliding step forwards.
4. A then takes gliding step forwards.
5. B follows with a gliding step backwards.
6. A takes a gliding step to the right.
7. B follows with a gliding step to the left.
8. A takes a gliding step to the left.
9. B follows with a gliding step to the right.

After practicing this for 1-2 minutes, change so that B leads and A follows. After that, this mirror drill can be done as a free exercise – shadowing each other.

1. A and B stand opposite each other. On the floor between them lies a medicine ball. Both stand far enough away from the ball so that they can't touch each other. Both now practice sparring by doing punches and steps without hitting the other person. The partner does the dodging, blocking and sweeping movements as realistically as possible in response to the punches lead by the other.

2.3   Games

Games considerably increase motivation beyond all measure, without people being conscious of their influence. This is particularly the case when you are dealing with children and youth. But grown-ups can be equally enthusiastic about them. Exercises that are not very popular, like falling down exercises can be 'wrapped up' into a game and when played they are found to no longer be unpleasant or boring.

Including games can make exercises more varied.

2.3.1   Catching Games

1
One player is the catcher. He can 'tag' the other players either with the hand or with the foot. The player can tag or kick back straight away.

2
One player is the catcher. His job is to knock all the other players out of the game. When he tags another player, that player has to get down on all fours to form a seat. He can be freed by other players by one of them crawling or slipping through underneath the arms and legs. If he is caught by the catcher as he does this, he also has to adopt the all fours position.

3
One player is the catcher. His job is to knock all the other players out of the game. When he tags another player, that player has to stand still and bend his body over at right angles. He can be freed by other players by one of them leapfrogging over his back. If he is caught by the catcher as he does this, he also has to stand still and adopt the same position as above.

4
One player is the catcher. The changeover takes place by the catcher tagging another player with his hand or leg. That player can free himself by completing one of the following exercises (as laid down by the instructor beforehand):

- Forward roll
- Backward roll
- Fall down sideways
- Fall down forwards
- Fall down backwards

When the exercise begins the catcher has to go off to chase another player.

5

The catcher is on all fours and is crawling along on the ground. His job is to make all the other players fall over. As soon as another player falls over he also becomes a catcher. The game ends when all the players have become catchers.

6

All the players – less two (the hunter and the hunted) are spread around the room and are squatting down. The hunter chases the hunted. If the hunted sits down next to one of the crouching players, then the roles are changed. The player crouching down now becomes the hunter and the player who was previously the hunter now becomes the hunted. Make sure that the roles change quickly.

7

All the players – except for two (the hunter and the hunted) are spread around the room and are lying down on their stomachs with the head pointing to the middle of the room. The hunter chases the hunted. If the hunted lies down next to one of the other players, then the roles are changed. The player originally lying down now becomes the hunter and the player who was previously the hunter now becomes the hunted. Make sure that the roles change quickly.

2.3.2   Fighting Games

#1

An area is marked out, either by using Judo mats or by laying down belts or pieces of clothing. All the players are inside this area. On a command all the players start to try to get the other players outside the area by throwing them or pushing them. If any part of a player's body is outside the area, then this counts as that player having to leave the area and be eliminated.

2

The players walk around in threes. One of them is the attacker, one the bodyguard and the third is the person being protected. The bodyguard is positioned in between the two others. The attacker tries to get past the bodyguard. The bodyguard can prevent this by only using his body and the extremities. The bodyguard cannot use his hands to get hold of the attacker. Play should not exceed 30 seconds. Then the bodyguard gives way and the attacker gets hold of the person being protected and throws him onto the ground. Now they change roles.

3

The players take off their belts (if they are wearing them) and stick them into their pants at the back. If people aren't wearing belts they can use clothes pegs. On a command each player tries to steal the belt (clothes peg). When a player loses it then he is out.

4

The players walk around in pairs. One of them lies down on his stomach. The other partner has to now try to turn the other partner over onto his back. The one lying on his stomach tries to make this difficult by squirming about and stretching out his legs and arms to stop it happening.

5

Two groups are formed. Each group nominates a 'King'. Each group has to try and abduct the 'King' from the other group and move him over to the other group. The group that manages to abduct the 'King' to the other group first is the winner. The 'King' must not do anything to prevent this happening. The group owning the 'King' may hold him firm or sit on him to prevent the abduction. Each group has to decide between using their manpower to abduct the 'King' or save them to protect their own 'King'.

6

The players walk around in pairs. They should both be of about the same size. On a command they carry out groundwork fighting. The instructor will give the end-position to be achieved, so if he calls 'on top' then the mount position must be achieved. On the command 'underneath' the one must be lying underneath the opponent. The instructor can extend the game by selecting various different positions (mount, cross-over, leg scissors, scarf hold etc.).

7

The players walk around in pairs. They should both be of about the same size. On a command they carry out groundwork fighting. The players have to play using the following rules:

- Both are blindfolded.
- Both of them have their legs tied together (e.g., using a belt).
- Both of then have the hands tied together (e.g., using a belt).
- One arm is pinned to the side using a belt.
- One of them has his hands tied together while the other has his feet tied together.
- One of them is blindfolded while the other has his hands or feet tied together.

8

The players walk around in pairs. They should both be of about the same size. On a command they carry out groundwork fighting. The aim is to get the belt off the other player.

9

The players walk around in pairs. They should both be of about the same size. On a command they carry out groundwork fighting. One of the players is holding an object (e.g., a ball) that he has to hold on to. The other partner has to try to get the object off the other one. Once the ball has been won or a certain time has been exceeded then the roles are changed over.

10

The players crawl around on all fours in pairs. Each one of the partners tries to sweep the other's hands away to make him fall down onto his chest.

11

The players walk around in pairs. Both of them spar against each other. They try to hit the other on the head or a certain part of the body with the flat of the hand (slap). At the same time the other partner has to watch that he keeps his guard up.

12

The players walk around in pairs. They should both be of about the same size. One of the partners jumps up and clasps his legs around the other's hips. He now has to try to crawl once around the other's body without a leg touching the ground. This game can be varied with other forms of action, for example, climb over the head or between the legs.

2.4 Exercise Forms/Drills for Punching and Kicking While Standing

The following drills should be done for 2 minutes followed by a break for 1 minute.

1. A and B are standing opposite each other with their left legs leading and with their arms raised to form a guard.

2. A does a left-fisted jab at B's head. B blocks the jab with the inside of his right hand.

3. B does a left-fisted jab at A's head and A blocks the jab with the inside of his right hand.

1. A and B are standing opposite each other with their left legs leading and with their arms raised to form a guard.
2. A does a right-fisted cross at B's head. B blocks the cross with the inside of his right hand.
3. B does a right-fisted cross at A's head and A blocks the cross with the inside of his right hand.

1. A and B are standing opposite each other with their left legs leading and with their arms raised to form a guard.
2. B does a left-fisted jab at A's head. A ducks . . .
3. . . . stabilizes his position and does a left-fisted jab at B's head. B ducks underneath this.

1. A and B are standing opposite each other with their left legs leading and with their arms raised to form a guard.
2. B does a right-fisted cross at A's head. A ducks . . .
3. . . . stabilizes his position and does a right-fisted cross at B's head. B ducks underneath this.

1. A and B are standing opposite each other with their left legs leading and with their arms raised to form a guard.
2. B does a left-fisted punch at A's head. A sweeps the punch away to the inside with the inside of the right hand.
3. A does a left-fisted punch at B's head. B sweeps the punch away to the inside with the inside of the right hand . . .

1. A and B are standing opposite each other with their left legs leading and with their arms raised to form a guard.

2. B does a right-fisted cross at A's head. A rolls his left shoulder in front of his chin to prevent the punch hitting his chin.

3. A does a right-fisted cross at B's head. B rolls his left shoulder in front of his chin to prevent the punch hitting his chin.

1. A and B are standing opposite each other with their left legs leading and with their arms raised to form a guard.

2. B does a right-fisted cross at A's head. A turns his head sharply to the rear to prevent the punch being effective . . .

3. . . . and turns his head back to the front. A does a right-fisted cross at B's head. B turns his head sharply to the rear to prevent the punch being effective . . .

1. A and B are standing opposite each other with their left legs leading and with their arms raised to form a guard.

2. B does a right-fisted cross at A's head. A turns his head sharply to the right...

3. ...and lowers his head down onto his chest...

4. ...and ducks underneath the punch, bringing his head back up again.

5. A does a right-fisted cross at B's head. B turns his head to the right...

6. ...and lowers his head down onto his chest...

7. ...and ducks under-neath the punch...

8. ...and brings his head back up again.

1. A and B are standing opposite each other with their arms raised to form a guard.

2. B executes his favorite punch. A blocks, ducks or sweeps this away.

3. Now A does his favorite punch. B is able to block, sweep this away or duck.

The punching sequence should be flowing and done without breaks.

1. A and B are standing opposite each other.

2. B executes his favorite leg kick technique. A blocks, ducks or sweeps this away.

3. Now A does his favorite leg kick technique. B is able to block, sweep this away or duck.

The kicking sequence should be flowing and done without breaks.

1. A and B are standing opposite each other. Both lead with their left leg.

2. B turns his left foot in (at least to right angles with A) and executes a lowkick at the outside of A's left thigh.

3. B does a gliding movement/lunge step inwards to the right so that he is standing in front of A.

4. A delivers a cross at B's head with his right fist...

5. ...then a hook at B's liver with his left fist...

6. ...and ends up with a cross at B's head.

7. A turns his left foot in (at least to right angles with B) and executes a lowkick at the outside of B's left thigh.

8. B does a gliding movement/lunge step inwards to the right so that he is standing in front of A.

9. B delivers a cross at A's head with his right fist . . .

10. . . . then a hook at A's liver with his left fist . . .

11. . . . and ends up with a cross at A's head.

From here on there is a changeover and A starts with his left leg.

1. A and B are standing opposite each other. Both lead with their left leg.

2. A turns his left foot in (at least to right angles with B) and executes a lowkick at the outside of B's left thigh.

3. B pulls his left leg to the rear...

4. ...and lets A's leg whiz past the target.

5. B does a lowkick at the rear of A's right leg.

Now changeover.

1. A and B are standing opposite each other. Both lead with their left leg.

2. A turns his left foot in (at least to right angles with B) and executes a lowkick at the outside of B's left thigh.

3. B pulls his left leg to the rear . . .

4. . . . and lets A's leg whiz past the target.

5. B does a lowkick at the rear of A's left thigh.

Now changeover.

1. A and B are standing opposite each other. Both lead with their left leg.

2. A turns his left foot in (at least to right angles with B) and executes a lowkick at the outside of B's left thigh.

3. B does a stop kick with his forward left foot against the thigh/groin of A's attacking leg.

4. B now places his left foot next to the inside of A's left foot ...

5. ... and sweeps it out to the right ...

6. ... places the left foot to the rear and concludes by executing a stamping action with his right leg at A's left knee.

Now change over.

1. A and B are standing opposite each other. Both lead with their left leg.

2. A turns his left foot in (at least to right angles with B) and executes a lowkick at the outside of B's left thigh. B does a stop kick with his forward left foot against the thigh/groin of A's attacking leg . . .

3. . . . and delivers a cross to the head with his right fist . . .

4. . . . followed by an uppercut to the head with his left fist . . .

5. . . . and then places his right leg to the rear . . .

6. . . . and executes a lowkick with the left leg at the inside of A's left thigh.

Now change over.

1. A and B are standing opposite each other. Both lead with their left leg.
2. A turns his left foot in (at least to right angles with B). At the same time B turns his right foot in (at least to right angles with A)
3. A executes a lowkick towards the outside of B's left thigh. By virtue of B's turning motion, however, A hits B's behind. At the same time as A does the lowkick, B also does a lowkick with his left leg at the inside of A's left thigh.

Now change over.

1. A and B are standing opposite each other. Both lead with their left leg.
2. A turns his left foot in (at least to right angles with B) and executes a lowkick at the outside of B's left thigh.

3. B takes a gliding step/lunge inwards to the right so that he is always standing in front of A and as he does this, he grabs hold of A's right leg in his left hand. B places his right hand on A's right shoulder so that A cannot use his right hand to punch. B drops his head so that his chin is protected underneath his own right upper arm.

4. B does a knee kick with his right leg against A's right thigh . . .

5. . . . then places his right leg to the rear . . .

6. . . . and delivers another knee kick with his right knee . . .

7. . . . places his right leg to the rear again . . .

8. . . . turns his left foot in and ends the combination with a lowkick at A's left knee.

Now change over.

1. A and B are standing opposite each other. Both lead with their left leg.

2. A turns his left foot in (at least to right angles with B) and executes a highkick at the height of B's left rib-cage. B counters by doing a passive block downwards and grabs hold of A's right lower leg in his right hand . . .

3. . . . and pushes A's right leg down directly towards the ground so that A is standing with all his weight on the right leg.

4. B then turns his right leg in . . .

5. . . . and ends the combination with a lowkick at the rear of A's right thigh.

Now change over.

2.5　Exercise Forms/Drill at Trapping Range

2.5.1　Hubud (Rhythm Drill & Defense Sequence)

This training method trains one for sharpness, timing, speed and coordination at close reach.

1. A delivers a right-arm punch at angle #1 (inwards at the head) against B. As he does this A leans forward pushing slightly. B blocks the attacking arm with his left lower arm and gives way to the push being done by A by moving slightly to the rear...

2. ... and sweeps the attacking arm clockwise to the right...

3. ... taking hold of A's right arm around the elbow with his left hand. For this there are two possibilities:

   a　His thumb is lying on the upper arm.

   b　The thumb is underneath A's upper arm. The disadvantage of this method is that you cannot check the upper arm this way and as long as A tries to hit B's stomach with his right arm. This would be much more dangerous if knives were in play.

4. B now delivers a punch with his right fist at angle # 1 (inwards at the head) against A.

5. A sweeps the attacking arm clockwise to the right and takes hold of B's right arm around the elbow with his left hand. For this there are two possibilities:

   a His thumb is lying on the upper arm.

   b The thumb is underneath B's upper arm. The disadvantage of this method is that you cannot check the upper arm this way and as long as B tries to hit A's stomach with his right arm. This would be much more dangerous if knives were in play.

6. A delivers a punch with his right hand at angle #1 (inwards at the head) at B's head.

Roles are now changed over.

2.5.2 Bong-Sao - Lop Sao Rolling Defense Drill

1. A delivers a right-arm back-fisted punch at angle #2 (outwards at the head) against B. As he does this A leans forward pushing slightly. B blocks the attacking arm with his left lower arm (Bong Sao). As he does this B's hand is pointing towards the ground. The upper arm is held forward almost in a line with his own shoulder. The angle between his upper and lower arm is about 135°. The little finger of the left hand is pointing towards the ceiling.

2. B places his right hand on the back of A's right fist, sweeps A's right arm downwards and delivers a backhanded punch at A's head.

Now change over.

2.6   Exercise Forms/Drills at Grappling Range

2.6.1   Basic Escrima Drill

Note: In this exercise, the neck should not be held on to and the drill should be exercised gently.

1. A and B are standing opposite each other with each having his left arm pushed underneath the opposing arm.
2. Each now tries to get his right arm through inside the other's arm.
3. When each succeeds in doing this, the arms are stretched as if one could clasp the arms around the other's hips.
4. Each now tries to get his left arm through inside the other's arm.
5. When each succeeds in doing this, the arms are stretched as if one could clasp the arms around the other's hips.

The drill starts all over again.

2.6.2 Further Exercise Forms/Drills

1. A and B are standing opposite each other with each holding on to the other's opposing left wrist.

2. A grabs hold of B's left wrist with his left hand . . .

3. . . . moves to B's left side . . .

4. . . . and clasps him around his back.

Whoever manages to do this first gets a point.

If the opponents have difficulty working together, here are a few alternatives.

Example 1:

1. A has to push B back over a certain line.
2. If A manages this he gets a point (Picture 1 and 2).

However, if B manages to get around behind A's back, then B gets the point.

Note: This drill has an advantage in the warming up session because it is also representative of the fighting competition.

Example 2:

B has fixed a belt/band around A's upper body and is holding it firmly in both hands. Now A tries to pull away from the belt holding him back.

The following drill aims to speed up the action of taking control of the opponent's head. It is also used to strengthen the neck muscles.

1. A and B are standing opposite each other with each holding on to the other's neck with both of their hands. The hands are clasped over each other so that the fingers are not bunched up. B's left hand is lying over his right hand and A's right hand is lying over his left one. Both try to pull the other's head forward while each tenses his neck muscles to prevent this happening.

2. B feeds his right hand through under A's left arm . . .

3. . . . and grabs hold of A's neck.

4. Then B feeds his left hand similarly through under A's right arm . . .

5. . . . and grabs hold of his neck.

6. A feeds his right hand through under B's left arm . . .

7. . . . and grabs hold of B's neck.

8. Then A feeds his left hand similarly through under B's right arm . . .

9. . . . and grabs hold of his neck.

1.   A and B are standing opposite each other. A is holding on to B's neck with both hands. The hands are clasped over each other so that the fingers are not bunched up. B's arms are held up as a guard.

2.-3.   A pulls B's neck forward with both of his arms and does twists and turns at the same time. While this is going on, B is punching away at A's stomach.

1. A and B are standing opposite each other. A is holding on to B's neck with his right hand. B places his left hand over A's right arm.

2. B sweeps A's right hand outwards and away with his right hand . . .

3. . . . brings his left hand up in the direction of the right side of A's throat . . .

4. . . . and grabs hold of A's neck with his left hand.

5. A strikes B's left arm to one side with his left hand . . .

6. . . . brings his right hand up in the direction of the left side of A's throat . . .

7. . . . and grabs hold of B's neck.

2.6.3 Exercise Forms/Drills on the Ground

1. A is on top of B in the mount position.

2. B is pinning A's right arm to his chest using both arms . . .

3. . . . and grabs hold of A's neck with his left hand and lifts his hips up . . .

4. . . . and rolls him over his left shoulder. A is holding B in the guard position (kidney-scissor grip) . . .

5. . . . and places his right elbow below A's left knee . . .

6. . . . and presses A's left leg down on to the ground . . .

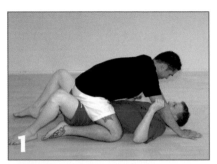

7. . . . brings his left leg over A's left thigh . . .

8. . . . and moves around into the sideways cross position . . .

9. . . . moves his leg that was pinning the leg . . .

10. . . . and adopts the reverse side mount, pinning down A's right leg with his left hand . . .

11. . . . and then he brings his left leg over A's legs . . .

12. . . . and adopts the mount position.

Now change over.

1. A is on top of B in the frontal side mount position (Kesa Gatame/scarf hold) and has pushed his right arm around B's neck.

2. B turns towards A and brings both of his arms around A's upper body and clasps his hands together...

3. ... and pulls A upwards...

4. ... and further around clockwise to the left.

5. B now adopts the frontal side mount position.

6. A now turns towards B and brings both of his arms around B's upper body and clasps his hands together . . .

7. . . . and pulls B upwards . . .

8. . . . and further around clockwise to the left.

9. A now adopts the frontal side mount position.

Now change over.

1. B is on top of A in the mount position. Both of A's arms are underneath B's upper body.
2. A pushes B upwards with both arms.
3. B brings his left leg first of all forwards . . .
4. . . . and then places it over A's head . . .
5. . . . and then himself drop backwards. B is holding A's arm in both hands pinned between his legs. A uses the impetus of B's backwards motion and sits up . . .
6. . . . coming into kneeling position and pulls his right arm back . . .

7. . . . and moves around onto B's right side, placing his left hand down beside the left hand side of B's head and pushes B's legs down away from his left shoulder . . .

8. . . . brings his head backwards and dodges B's legs as they whiz past his head. A pins both of B's legs down with his right arm.

9. A is now in the reverse side mount on top of B and is controlling B's left leg with his left hand.

10. A now brings his right leg over B's legs . . .

11. . . . and adopts the mount position.

Now change over.

2.7 Drills Using a Knife

Once the drills have been perfected, the intensity in which they are carried out can be increased. The movements with the knife should be carried out with full force. The aim is to strike the opponent with the exercise knife to make sure that he reacts quickly and with sufficient energy.

1. A and B are standing opposite each other and they are holding a knife in their right hands. (The knife is held on the thumb side, i.e. on top).

2. A strikes at angle # 1 (inwards towards the neck). B places his left hand on the outside of A's right hand . . .

3. . . . and sweeps A's right arm inwards . . .

4. . . . and then strikes using angle # 1 (inwards towards the neck). B places his right hand on the outside of A's left hand . . .

5. . . . and sweeps the right arm downwards . . .

6. . . . and then strikes using angle # 2 (outwards towards the neck). A places left hand on the outside of B's right hand . . .

7. . . . and sweeps the right arm downwards.

8. . . . and then strikes using angle # 2 (outwards towards the neck). B places left hand on the outside of A's right hand . . .

9. . . . and sweeps it downwards.

Now start the drill all over again.

After the drill has been perfected, the following variations of movements can be used:

- A and B take two steps forwards and then back again.

- A and B take two steps to the left and then back again to the right.

- A and B move around in a circle and then reverse back again around in a circle.

- A and B move around a square form (two steps backwards, two steps to the left, two steps forwards and two steps to the right).

1. A and B are standing opposite each other and they are holding a knife in their right hands. (The knife is held on the thumb side, i.e. on top).

2. A strikes at angle # 3 (inwards towards the stomach). B places his left hand on the outside of A's right hand . . .

3. . . . and sweeps A's right arm inwards . . .

4. . . . and then strikes using angle # 3 (inwards towards the stomach). B places his left hand on the outside of A's right hand . . .

5. . . . and sweeps the right arm inwards . . .

6. . . . and then strikes using angle # 4 (outwards towards the stomach). A places left hand on the outside of B's right hand . . .

7. . . . and sweeps this downwards . . .

8. . . . and then strikes using angle # 4 (outwards towards the stomach). B places his left hand on the outside of A's right hand . . .

9. . . . and sweeps this downwards.

10. B strikes using strike # 5 (directly at the stomach). A places his left hand on the outside of B's right hand . . .

11.-12. . . . and sweeps B's right arm inwards . . .

13. . . . and then does a strike using strike # 5 (directly at the stomach). B places his left hand on the outside of A's right hand . . .

14. . . . and sweeps this inwards.

Now start the drill all over again.

After Drills # 1 & # 2 have been perfected, the variations of movement can also be incorporated in these drills.

As a further step, the exercisers can freely choose the angles of attack to be used.

2.8 Increased Stress Levels in a Self-Defense Situation

The following exercises are aimed at placing the participant under stress so that he learns to react to real self-defense situations in a level-headed manner. While, on the one hand, these exercises increase stamina performance, on the other hand they also increase strength and speed performance.

When doing the exercises shown, the participants should wear protective equipment (genital protection, gum shields etc.).

Exercise # 1

Load time: Maximum of 2 minutes.

In this exercise, three people are active. A is holding two punch pads, B delivers the combination sequences against the punch pads while C is trying to interrupt the action.

C has an arm pad. He uses this to get in B's way as the latter tries to strike A's punch pads, or alternatively he uses them to strike B's upper body.

B has to get past C or push him to one side so that he can execute the combination sequence.

Exercise #2

Load time: Maximum of 2 minutes.

All the participants (except one) use an arm pad and stand in a circle. A is in the center of the circle and does not have an arm pad. On the trainer's command, all the people forming the circle start to move in to make the circle smaller so that the one in the center begins to feel hemmed in. The stress level can be increased when all of the players make a noise. On the trainer's next command, A tries to fight his way out of the circle and break out of it. The people in the circle try to prevent him from doing this. As soon as A has managed to break out of the circle a changeover takes place.

Exercise #3

Load time: Maximum of 2 minutes.

Form two teams for the following exercise. One of the teams has to have more players in it than the other. Both teams start sparring – team against team – using light actions. Members of each team have to watch each other in case they see one of their team in danger and need to go to his support.

The footwork of the sparring opponents does not have to be necessarily precise.

3   Stretching Exercises

3   Stretching Exercises

3.1   Neck Exercises

1. Stand, legs apart facing forwards with your head lifted up normally.
2. Drop your head down onto your chest . . .
3. . . . roll it around towards the right shoulder . . .
4. . . . up around into the center (don't let the head come back into the neck) . . .
5. . . . and over to the left side . . .
6. . . . and back into the center.

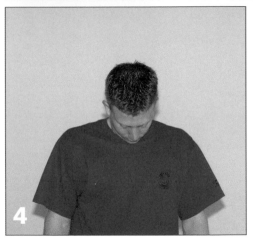
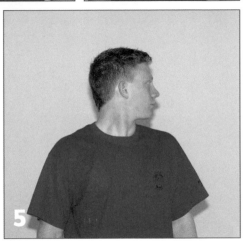

1. Stand, legs apart facing forwards with your head lifted up normally.
2. Drop your head down onto your chest . . .
3. . . . look over your right shoulder . . .
4. . . . bring your head back down to the center . . .
5. . . . and now look over the left shoulder.

1. Stand, legs apart facing forwards with your head lifted up normally.

2. Bring your head loosely a little to the right . . .

3. . . . and now move it over to the left as if you were shaking your head to say 'No!'.

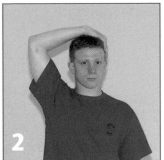

1. Stand, legs apart facing forwards with your head lifted up normally.

2. Place your right hand over your head onto your left ear...

3. ...and pull your head towards your right shoulder as you stretch your left arm towards the floor. Hold this position tensed for about three breaths.

4. Bring your head back to the center position. Place your left hand over your head onto your right ear...

5. ...and pull your head towards your left shoulder as you stretch your right arm towards the floor. Hold this position tensed for about three breaths.

3.2   Shoulder, Latissimus Dorsi and Chest Exercises

1.   Stand, legs apart facing forwards.

2.   Bring your arms, stretching them out and up from behind. The palms of the hands are pointing up to the ceiling.

3.   Bring the arms up into a 45° angle and hold them tensed for about three breaths and then let them go loose again.

Repeat the exercise 3 times.

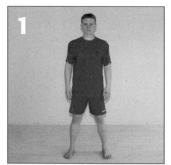

1.   Stand in front of your partner. Your partner is kneeling on one knee with his body upright.

2.   Place both your hands on his shoulders ...

3.   ... and bend your upper body, stretching your backbone. You can take the weight off your back by stretching one leg out to the rear.

Repeat this exercise twice. Place a different leg to the rear each time.

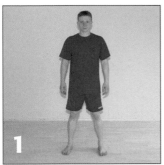

1. Stand, legs apart facing forwards.

2. Bring your right arm over in front of the left-hand side of your body...

3. ...place the left lower arm in front of your right upper arm near the elbow and pull the right arm towards your chest. Hold this position tensed for about three breaths and then relax again.

4. Bring your left arm over in front of the right-hand side of your body...

5. ...place the right lower arm in front of your left upper arm near the elbow and pull the left arm towards your chest. Hold this position tensed for about three breaths and then relax again.

Repeat this exercise 3 times each side.

1. Stand, legs apart facing forwards.

2. Bring your right hand back between your shoulder blades . . .

3. . . . place the left hand on the rear of the right upper arm near the right elbow and pull the right arm rearwards. Hold this position tensed for about three breaths and then relax again.

4. Bring your left hand back between your shoulder blades . . .

5. . . . place the right hand on the rear of the left upper arm near the left elbow and pull the left arm rearwards. Hold this position tensed for about three breaths and then relax again.

Repeat this exercise 3 times each side.

1. Stand, legs apart facing forwards.

2. Bring your right hand back between your shoulder blades . . .

3. . . . place the left hand on the rear of the right upper arm near the right elbow and pull the right arm to the left. Hold this position tensed for about three breaths and then relax again.

4. Bring your left hand back between your shoulder blades . . .

5. . . . place the right hand on the rear of the left upper arm near the left elbow and pull the left arm to the right. Hold this position tensed for about three breaths and then relax again.

Repeat this exercise 3 times each side.

1. Stand, legs apart facing forwards.
2. Bring your arms behind your back and clasp your hands together.
3. Bend your upper body forward and stretch your arms out up forwards towards your head as far as you can. Hold them tensed in this position for about three breaths and then relax again.

Repeat this exercise 3 times.

1. Stand sideways on to a wall, legs slightly apart facing forwards. The wall is on your right hand side.
2. Stretch your right arm out behind you against the wall. Turn your body slightly counterclockwise. Hold this position tensed for about three breaths and then relax again.
3. Turn around the other way and now place your left arm stretched out behind you against the wall. Turn your body slightly clockwise. Hold this position tensed for about three breaths and then relax again.

Repeat this exercise 3 times each side.

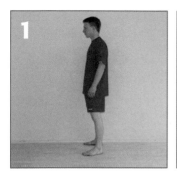
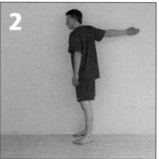

If there is no wall available, the exercise can be done as follows:

1. You are kneeling on all fours.
2. Stretch your right arm out to the right. Drop your right shoulder down onto the floor. Turn your upper body clockwise. The shoulder and the arm must stay on the floor. Hold this position tensed for about three breaths and then relax again.
3. You are kneeling on all fours.
4. Stretch your left arm out to the right. Drop your right shoulder down onto the floor. Turn your upper body counterclockwise. The shoulder and the arm must stay on the floor. Hold this position tensed for about three breaths and then relax again.

Repeat this exercise 3 times each side.

1. A is lying on his stomach with his arms bent down sideways. B is kneeling in front of A's head.

2. B takes hold of both of A's arms . . .

3. . . . and pulls them towards himself. A holds the position tensed for three breaths and then relaxes again.

Repeat this exercise 3 times.

3.3 Arm Exercises

1. Stand, legs apart facing forwards.

2. Stretch your right arm out with the palm of the right hand pointing upwards.

3. Take hold of the fingers and palm of your right hand in your left hand and pull them in the direction of your body. Hold this position tensed for about three breaths and then relax again.

4. Stretch your left arm out with the palm of the left hand pointing upwards.

5. Take hold of the fingers and palm of your left hand in your right hand and pull them in the direction of your body. Hold this position tensed for about three breaths and then relax again.

Repeat this exercise 3 times.

1. Stand, legs apart facing forwards.

2. Place both of the palms of your hands together . . .

3. . . . push your arms downwards without the palms of your hands losing contact and hold this position tensed for about three breaths and then relax again.

Repeat this exercise 3 times.

3.4   Hand Exercises

Note: The following exercise can be done also when standing.
1.   You are sitting down on your heels.
2.   Turn your right hand in a clockwise direction.
3.   Take hold of the ball of the thumb of your right hand in your left hand . . .
4.   . . . and pull the right hand downwards.
5.   In this position twist the right hand forwards and hold this position tensed for about three breaths and then relax again.
6.   Turn your left hand in a clockwise direction.
7.   Take hold of the ball of the thumb of your left hand in your right hand . . .
8.   . . . and pull the left hand downwards.
9.   In this position twist the left hand forwards and hold this position tensed for about three breaths and then relax again.
Repeat this exercise 3 times.

Note: The following exercise can be done also when standing.

1. You are sitting down on your heels.

2. Turn your right hand in a counterclockwise direction.

3. Take hold of the back of your right hand in your left hand . . .

4. . . . and pull the right hand towards your upper body. Hold this position tensed for about three breaths and then relax again.

5. Turn your left hand in a counterclockwise direction.

6. Take hold of the back of your left hand in your right hand . . .

7. . . . and pull the left hand towards your upper body. Hold this position tensed for about three breaths and then relax again.

Repeat this exercise 3 times.

Note: The following exercise can be done also when standing.

1. You are sitting down on your heels.

2. Place your right elbow onto your right thigh.

3. Take hold of the back of your right hand in your left hand. Bend your right hand downwards. Hold this position tensed for about three breaths and then relax again.

4. Place your left elbow onto your left thigh.

5. Take hold of the back of your left hand in your right hand. Bend your left hand downwards. Hold this position tensed for about three breaths and then relax again.

Repeat this exercise 3 times.

3.5 Exercises for the Back

1. Adopt a position kneeling on all fours.

2. Stretch your right arm sideways up to the right. Follow the right arm with your eyes.

3. Bring your right arm back down again and place it through behind your propped up left arm.

4. Place your right arm back in its original position.

5. Stretch your left arm sideways up to the left. Follow the left arm with your eyes.

6. Bring your left arm back down again and place it through behind your propped up right arm.

7. Place your left arm back in its original position.

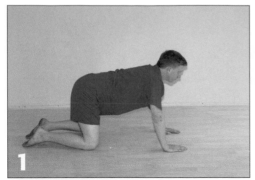

1. Adopt a position kneeling on all fours.
2. Stretch your right arm up while stretching your left leg out to the rear horizontally. Hold this position tensed for about 10 seconds.
3. Adopt a position kneeling on all fours.
4. Stretch your left arm up while stretching your right leg out to the rear horizontally. Hold this position tensed for about 10 seconds.
5. Adopt a position again kneeling on all fours.

1. Adopt a position kneeling on all fours.

2. Stretch both of your arms as far forward as possible. Drop your bottom onto your heels as you do this.

3. Bring your bottom back up again until the thighs are at right angles to the floor.

1. Lie down on your back and bring your legs up with the heels of your feet still on the floor.

2. Lay your knees over to the left side. Make sure that as you do this you don't twist your upper body with the movement.

3. Bring your knees back into the center . . .

4. . . . and lay your knees over to the right side.

1. Lie down on your back and bring your legs up with the heels of your feet still on the floor.

2. Lift your bottom slowly upwards so that your spine is free of the floor and hold this position for a short while.

3. Let your bottom slowly sink downwards again until your spine – vertebrae for vertebrae – is touching the floor.

1.   Lie down on your back and bring your legs up with the heels of your feet still on the floor.

2.   Lift your bottom slowly upwards so that your spine is free of the floor.

3.   Hold this position and bring your weight onto your right leg. Now stretch your left leg out until both thigh and lower leg form a straight line. Put your leg back down again and then do the exercise again using the right leg.

1. Lie down on your back . . .

2. . . . and lift your upper body forward and grab around your shins (close to the knees) with both of your arms. Try to touch your knees with your head. Try to hold this position tensed for about 20 seconds.

1. Lie down on your back and lay your arms down on the floor close to your body.

2. Bring your knees up so that your legs are angled . . .

3. . . . and bring them up backwards over your head. Make sure you keep your arms on the floor. In this position lift your head up.

4. Return to the start position.

1. Lie down on your back and lay your arms down on the floor close to your body.

2. Bring your legs up in the direction of your head and at the same time lift your head up towards your chest.

1. Lie down on your back . . .

2. . . . and push both of your hands underneath your bottom and lift both legs up.

3.-4. In this position do cycling movements with your legs. Do this for about 90 seconds.

1. Lie down on your back . . .

2. Stretch your arms out to the sides at right angles . . .

3. . . . bring your legs up so that your thighs are at right angles to your upper body and your lower legs are at right angles to your thighs (as if you are sitting on a chair).

4. Lay your knees over to the left side. Make sure that as you do this you don't twist your upper body with the movement. The knees should come to just short of touching the floor.

5. Bring your bent legs back into the center . . .

6. . . . and lay your knees over to the right side.

1. Lie down on your back . . .

2. . . . and stretch your right arm out to the side at a right angle . . .

3. . . . bend your right leg at the knee. Your head is turned to the side where your outstretched arm is.

4. Place your left arm on the outside of your right knee . . .

5. . . . and press your bent right leg over to the left side. Hold the tension for about 20 seconds. Now do this exercise again using the other leg.

1. Stand, legs apart facing forwards.

2. Bend your upper body forwards and place your hands on your shins.

3. Now 'crawl' your hands down your legs and along your feet until your hands touch the floor. As you do this exercise, breathe slowly and deeply out. Make sure your legs stay stretched.

4. With your hands, 'crawl' back up your feet and legs . . .

5. . . . and end up by lifting your body up straight again.

1. Stand leaning against a wall with your legs apart facing forwards.

2. Slowly slip your back down the wall until your thighs are at right angles to your lower legs (i.e. like a sitting position).

3. In this position stretch your arms upwards and out to the sides. Hold this position for about 20 seconds.

1. Stand, legs apart facing forwards.

2. Grab hold of your right knee in both hands . . .

3. . . . and pull it up to your chest. Repeat this with your other leg.

3.6   Stomach Exercises

1. You are lying on your stomach. Your hands are placed up next to your head. Your legs are together with the flats of the feet pointing upwards.

2. Push your upper body up by stretching your arms. Hold the position tensed for about three breaths.

3. Slowly lower your upper body down again.

1. You are lying on your back

2. Stretch your arms up behind your head as far as possible and press your legs down on to the floor. Hold the position tensed for about three breaths.

3.7 Hip Exercises

1. Stand, legs shoulder-width apart facing forwards.

2.-4. Swivel your hips around in a clockwise direction. After a while, change direction.

1. Stand, legs shoulder-width apart facing forwards.

2. Push your hips forward and hold this position for about three breaths.

3.8   Leg Exercises

1.   Squat down between your legs.

2.   Lean your upper body as far backwards as possible, supporting it with your hands. Hold this position for about three breaths.

1.   Lie down on your left side.

2.   Bend your right leg. Grab hold of your right foot in your right hand and pull this towards your bottom.

3.   Push your right hip forwards and hold this position tensed for about three breaths.

This exercise can be also done in a kneeling position.

1. Place your right leg forwards and kneel down on your left knee.
2. Bend your left leg up backwards and grab hold of it in your left hand and pull it towards your bottom.
3. Push your right hip forward and hold this position tensed for about three breaths.

Advanced exercisers can also do the exercise standing.

1. Stand, legs apart facing forwards.
2. Bend your left leg up backwards and grab hold of it in your left hand.
3. Pull your left leg towards your bottom and push your hips forward and hold this position tensed for about three breaths.

1. Sit down on the ground with your knees and legs angled outwards. The soles of the feet are touching each other.

2. Grab hold of your feet in your hands and pull them towards you as far as your can.

3. Place your elbows on your lower legs and press your elbows against them in the direction of the floor. Bend your upper body as far forward as possible towards the floor.

For advanced exercisers as a partner exercise.

1. Sit down on the ground with your knees and legs angled outwards. The soles of the feet are touching each other.

2. Grab hold of your feet in your hands and pull them towards you as far as you can. Your partner is standing behind you and first places his left foot . . .

3. . . . and then his right foot on your thighs. Hold this position tensed for about three breaths.

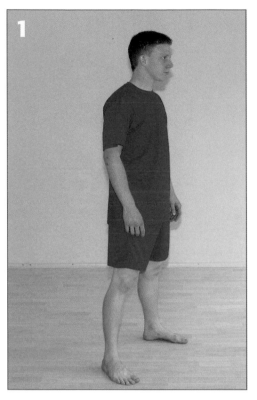

1. Stand, legs shoulder-width apart facing forwards.

2. Do the side-splits as far as you can. Push your hips forward and hold this position for three breaths.

1. Stand, legs shoulder-width apart facing forwards.

2. Do the side-splits as far as you can. Place your hands forward supporting you off the ground.

3. Bring your knees down on to the floor. Angle your lower legs roughly at right angles to your thighs.

4. Push your upper body to the rear and hold this position tensed for about three breaths.

5. Bring your upper body back forwards again and relax the tension.

1. Stand, legs shoulder-width apart facing forwards.
2. Do the side-splits. Place your hands forward supporting you off the ground.
3. Push your hips to the right and angle your right knee until it is over your right foot. Hold this position tensed for about three breaths.
4. Push your hips to the left and angle your left knee until it is over your left foot. Hold this position tensed for about three breaths.

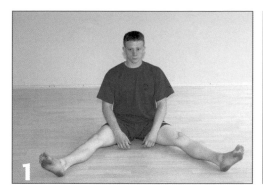

1. Sit down on the ground and stretch your legs out as far as possible in a 'V'.

2. Place both hands on the ground behind your thighs and push your hips forward. Hold this position tensed for about three breaths.

1. Sit down on the ground and stretch your legs out as far as possible in a 'V'.

2. Bring your upper body forward. Hold this position tensed for about three breaths.

3. Now bring your upper body from this position over towards your right leg and hold this position tensed for about three breaths.

4. Then bring your upper body from this position over towards your left leg and hold this position tensed for about three breaths.

5. Finally, bring your upper body from this position back into the center and hold this position tensed for about three breaths.

The last two exercises can be done as an exercise with a partner.

1. A and B are sitting down opposite each other and each has his legs spread out wide. B's feet are placed on the inside of A's ankles. They hold hands.

2. With his upper body remaining upright, B pulls A with both of his arms towards him and holds the position tensed for three breaths.

4. They now change the position of their feet . . .

5. . . . and A pulls B towards him and holds the position tensed for three breaths.

1. A and B are standing opposite each other. B kneels down . . .

2. . . . so that A can lay his straight right leg (foot angled normally forwards) on B's left shoulder.

3. B takes hold of A's right hand with his right hand. B stands up slowly until A gives a signal that the tension is sufficient. A holds the leg tensed for about three breaths. It is important that A stretches up from the knee and that his foot is stretched forward. A must keep looking at B.

4. B pulls back a little so that the tension on A's leg is increased. A gives a signal as soon as he finds the tension still acceptable. A holds the tension for about three breaths.

5. B returns first of all into the kneeling position . . .

6. . . . lowering his body slowly so that B can easily take his leg off B's shoulder.

Next, B does the exercise with his right leg. As soon as both have completed the exercise with their right legs, they do the exercise with their left legs.

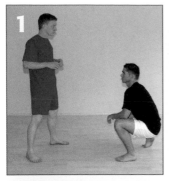

1.   A and B are standing opposite each other. B kneels down . . .

2.   . . . so that A can lay his straight right leg (foot angled sideways) sideways on B's left shoulder. B takes hold of A's right hand with his right hand.

3.   B stands up slowly until A gives a signal that the tension is sufficient. A holds the leg tensed for about three breaths. A makes sure that the hips are pulled inwards and that he stretches up from the knee and that his foot is stretched sideways (as if a sideways kick was being executed). A must keep looking at B.

4.   B pulls back a little so that the tension on A's leg is increased. A gives a signal as soon as he finds the tension still acceptable. A holds the tension for about three breaths.

5.   B returns first of all into the kneeling position . . .

6.   . . . lowering his body slowly so that B can easily take his leg off B's shoulder.

Next, B does the exercise with his right leg. As soon as both have completed the exercise with their right legs, they do the exercise with their left legs.

1. Sit down on the floor. Your upper body is upright and your legs are stretched out in front of you.

2. Bend your right leg and place your right ankle onto your left thigh. Pull your foot as far as possible in the direction of your left hip.

3. Place the right hand on your right knee and press it downwards. Hold the tensed position for about three breaths.

1. Lie down on your back and lift your legs up, bent at the knee, into a right angle.

2. Place your hands on the insides of your thighs near your knees.

3. Press your thighs outwards with both hands and hold the tensed position for about three breaths.

This exercise can also be done with a partner.

1. Lie down on your back and lift your legs up, bent at the knee, into a right angle. Your partner places both of his hands on the insides of your thighs near your knees.

2. Your partner presses your thighs outwards with both hands and you hold the tensed position for three breaths.

3. Stretch your legs out. Your partner pushes them in the direction of your upper body and you hold the tensed position for about three breaths.

3.9   Calf Exercises

1. Stand against a wall supported by both of your hands. Your right leg is placed forward and the left leg is to the rear.

2. Put the heel of your rear leg down onto the ground and push your left hip forwards.

Now do the exercise with the other leg.

1. Stand against a wall supported by both of your hands. Your right leg is placed forward and the left leg is to the rear. The toes of your right foot are pulled up angled.

2. Push the weight of your body to the rear until you can feel the tension in your right calf.

Now do the exercise with the other leg.

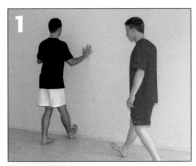

1. Sit down on the floor. Your legs are stretched out in front of you.

2. Bend your right leg and place the sole of your right foot at about the height of the knee.

3. Get hold of the toes of your left foot with your left hand and pull it towards you.

Now do the exercise using the other leg.

1. Sit down on the floor. Your legs are stretched out in front of you.

2. Bend your right leg and place the sole of your right foot at about the height of the knee.

3. Get hold of the toes of your left foot with your right hand and pull it towards you.

Now do the exercise using the other leg.

1. Sit down on the floor. Your legs are stretched out in front of you.

2. Bend your right leg and place the sole of your right foot at about the height of the knee.

3. Twist and bend your upper body in the direction of your left leg. Get hold of the toes of your left foot with your right hand and pull it towards you.

Now do the exercise using the other leg.

3.10   Foot Exercises

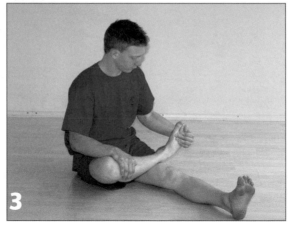

1.   Sit down on the floor. Your legs are stretched out in front of you.

2.   Bend your right leg and lay it over your left leg.

3.   Get hold of the toes of your right foot with your left hand and first twist the foot forwards and then in the other direction.

Now repeat the exercise using the other foot.

3.11   Toe Exercises

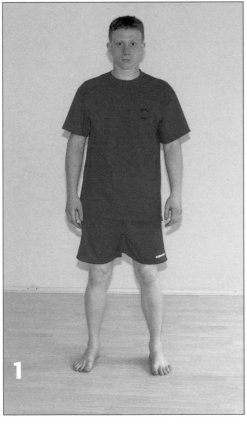

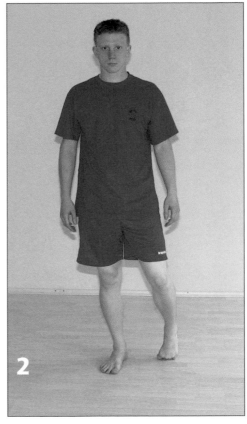

1.   Stand, legs apart facing forwards.

2.   Roll the toes of your left foot over the ground.

Now repeat the exercise using the other foot.

4 Relaxing

4.1 Autogenic Training (Schultz Method)

The use of the Schultz Method of Autogenic Training is very suitable to reduce anxiety and allow one to change various behavioral patterns. In order for it to be effective, weeks of practice are necessary. The first exercises (the heavy feeling) aim to make the body feel heavy and relaxed. The 'patient' repeatedly allows himself to think that his body feels heavy. "My body is heavy." To achieve this state, the 'patient' has to imagine that his body is being pulled down by several heavy weights attached to it.

The second exercise (a feeling of warmth) is about getting the right arm (for left-handers – the left arm) to feel warm. To study the technique further, there is ample comprehensive literature available.

To practice this, the 'patient' sits in a chair in a relaxed bent position, or, alternatively he lies down (e.g., on a bed). Now, the 'patient' lets the phrase, "I'm completely calm and relaxed," run through his mind. This is done together with controlled breathing. The beginner then thinks to himself, "My right arm is quite warm." You could also think about the blood flowing through your arm. The fact that a part of your body is warm can also be proved, by weighing it. By virtue of the assimilation of the idea into the brain, indeed more blood is 'pumped' into the part of the body and it becomes heavy. Now, you have to control your breathing. You do this by repeating several times, "My breathing is calm and even." Maybe you have already noticed that the key phrases are always formulated in a positive sense. For example, if you want to lose weight, you should not think, "Fat is bad for me." It would be better to think, "I like salad."

Most martial arts sportsmen and women know what the solar plexus is and that it is part of the central nervous system – like the sun at the center of our body's galaxy. A blow at this spot can lead to unconsciousness. We can imagine how the sun's rays shine on this spot (just above the stomach) and think to ourselves, "The sun's rays are warm." You will note that the spot is indeed warm when you manage to perfect the exercises above.

After completing the exercise with the solar plexus successfully (generally, each step needs about a week's training every day), then you can move on to learning to slow your heart rate down. You achieve this by repeating the key phrase, "My heart is quiet and beats evenly." With the following exercise you can conclude the basic training. The key phrase is "My forehead is pleasantly cool" (as always, note the positiveness). It is important to avoid saying, "My forehead is cold." This can cause strong headaches.

Once you have achieved the required level of relaxation, you can start using other key phrases, such as for example, "I'm going to do it"; "I'm hard-working" or, "It is quiet and calm, everywhere and all the time." Key phrases along these lines can be found in the book by Johannes H. Schultz (1884-1970) – "Autogenic Therapy."

It must be mentioned that after ending the exercises, you don't simply just open your eyes and stand up. This could cause headaches or other unpleasant feelings that are present for days on end. As soon as you have finished thinking about the key phrase and want to 'resurface' again, you must do this slowly and in a controlled manner. Quite often, one will ease themselves into the 'trance' by counting to ten, and exit by counting backwards from ten. An example of the latter is as follows:

10 I am counting down from 10 to 0 and am going to 'wake up' slowly.
9 I am now moving my feet . . .
8 . . . and now my arms.
7 I am now tensing my legs . . .
   .
   .
1 am now going to open my eyes and feel awake and refreshed.
0 (Eyes are open) – I am awake and refreshed.

What use is autogenic training for the sportsman? The key phrases should begin to show themselves in respective situations so that, for example, eating habits or feelings of anxiety are changed (of course – for the better). I am convinced of its effectiveness and recommend that you look into this subject in more depth.

4.2   Progressive Muscle Relaxation (Jacobsen Method)

Another method of relaxing is Jacobsen's progressive muscle relaxation method. This method can be put to good use after an intensive training session in order to relax the muscles.

Similarly, there are lots of reference works available that go into the subject more comprehensively. The following is just an introduction to the method.

Sequence:

1. Lie down on your back and try to become calm by breathing slowly and deeply. Close your eyes and let your arms rest down the sides of your body.

2. Clench both of your hands into a fist and tense the upper arms as hard as you can. Hold the tension and count to yourself up to 15.

3. Let the tension go and slowly unclench your fists. Try not to move your arms from now on.

4. Pull your shoulders up to your ears and hold them tensed while you count up slowly to 15.

5. Let the tension go and let your shoulders slowly sink back down again and try not to move them again.

6. Lift your head up and forward until you feel the tension in your neck. Hold your head tensed and slowly count up to 15.

7. Let the tension go and let your head sink slowly back down again. Try not to move your head again from now on.

8. Squeeze your eyelids closed as firmly as you can and open your mouth wide until your chin begins to tremble. Hold the position tensed and slowly count up to 15.

9. Let the tension go and note how your face relaxes.

10. Hollow your back and tense your back muscles. Hold this position tensed and slowly count to 15.

11. Let the tension go and lay your back down again. Try not to move your back from now on.

12. Breathe deeply from your stomach so that it is tense. Hold this position tensed and again slowly count to 15.

13. Let the tension go and breathe out deeply. Try not to let your stomach tense up any more from now on.

14. Tense the muscles of your bottom and hold them tensed. Slowly count up to 15.

15. Let the tension go and let your bottom drop down onto the bed. Try not to tense your bottom any more.

16. Tense your thighs and hold the position. Slowly count up to 15.

17. Let the tension go and let your thighs relax again onto the bed. Try not to move your thighs or tense them any more.

18. Stretch your feet out and tense your calf muscles. Hold them tense and slowly count up to 15.

19. Let the tension go and let your calf muscles relax slowly back onto the bed.

Appendix

Literature

Braun, C. (2005). *Jiu-Jitsu – the basics*. Maidenhead: Meyer & Meyer.

Braun, C. (2006). *Jiu-Jitsu – Training*. Maidenhead: Meyer & Meyer.

Braun, C. (2006). *Self-Defence against knife attacks*. Maidenhead: Meyer & Meyer.

Braun, C. (2006). *Grappling. Effective groundwork*. Maidenhead: Meyer & Meyer.

Braun, C. (2008). *Free fight – the ultimate guide to no holds barred fighting*. Maidenhead: Meyer & Meyer.

Braun, C. (2009). *Self defense*. Maidenhead: Meyer & Meyer.

DVDs

(in German, more information and ordering possibilities: **www.fight-academy.eu**)

Braun, C. (2006).
Selbstverteidigung gegen Messerangriffe – Street Safe Workshop: itf-multimedia

Braun, C. (2006).
Selbstverteidigung gegen Messerangriffe – Basics: itf-multimedia

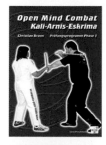

Braun, C. (2007).
Selbstverteidigung für Frauen – Basics: itf-multimedia

Braun, C. (2007).
Selbstverteidigung gegen Kontaktangriffe – Basics: itf-multimedia

Braun, C. (2007).
Selbstverteidigung gegen Messerangriffe – Entwaffnungstechniken – Workshop: itf-multimedia

Braun, C. (2007).
Open Mind Combat Prüfungsprogramm zur Phase I: itf-multimedia

Braun, C. (2007).
Selbstverteidigung gegen Stockangriffe – Basics: itf-multimedia

Braun, C. (2007).
Hebeltechniken – Basics: itf-multimedia

Braun, C. (2007).
Energydrills – Basics Energydrills – Advanced: itf-multimedia

Braun, C. (2007).
Doppelstockdrills / Sinawalis: itf-multimedia

About the Author

Christian Braun b. 1965

Profession:
Systems Analyst/IT Trainer/Author and Owner
of a Sports School

Address:
Peter-Paul-Rubens-Str. 1
67227 Frankenthal
E-Mail: Christian.Braun@fight-academy.eu
Homepage: www.fight-academy.eu

Requests for information regarding private and general courses,
martial arts books, training knives, sticks, protective goggles
and martial arts accessories should be sent to the above address.

Training Address:
Fight Academy Christian Braun
Westendstrasse 15
67059 Ludwigshafen
Tel: +49 / 1 77 / 2 84 30 80
E-Mail: Christian.Braun@fight-academy.eu
Homepage: www.fight-academy.eu

Qualifications:
- Head Instructor Open Mind Combat (OMC)
- 7th Dan Ju-Jitsu (All Japan Ju-Jitsu International Federation – AJJIF). 5th Dan Ju-Jutsu (German Ju-Jutsu Association), Licensed JJ-Instructor, Trainer 'B' License
- Phase 6 and Madunong Guro in the IKAEF under Jeff Espinous and Johan Skalberg
- Instructor in Progressive Fighting Systems (Jeet Kune Do Concepts) under Paul Vunak
- Instructor in Luta-Livre License Grade 1 under Andreas Schmidt
- 1st Dan Jiu-Jitsu (German Jiu-Jitsu Association)
- Phase 2 Jun Fan Gung Fu under Ralf Beckmann

Personal Security Guard Trainer:
- Trainer for personal security guards.

Offices held:
- Technical Director of the AJJIF in Germany
- 1990-1991 – Trainer and Press Representative for the Ju-Jutsu Section of the Judo
- Association for the German State of the Pfalz (Rhineland Palatinate)
- 1999-2003 – Speaker for the Ju-Jutsu Association (Ju-Jutsu Verband Baden e.V.) in matters for Sport for Seniors and the Disabled
- May 1992 - April 2006 – Head of Section in the Turn- und Gefechtclub 1861 e.V. (German Gymnastics and Fencing Club 1861)

Organization:
- Speaker on the German National Seminar of the DJJV e.V. (German Ju-Jutsu Association) 2003 and 2004
- Member of the Ju-Jutsu-Leitbildkommission (German Jiu Jitsu Steering Committee) for the DJJV e.V
- Speaker at German National Courses held by the DJJV e.V.
- Speaker in the faculty of JJ Instructors Division of the DJJV e.V.
- Member of the Trainer Team of the Ju-Jutsu Verband Baden e.V.
- Member of the Trainer Team of the DJJV e.V. in the faculty for Sport for the Disabled

Competition Achievements in the Upper Open Weight Classes:
Between 1988-1991 several place results achieved in the Pfalz Individual Championships with 1st Place taken in 1991. Placed in Third Place, three times in the German South-West Individual Championships. 2004, placed in Fourth Place in the Lock and Choke Tournament of the European Luta-Livre-Organization in the Upper Open Weight Class. In January 2005 in Karlsruhe, placed in Second Place in the Submissao Grappling Challenge. In February 2005 in Cologne, placed in Second Place in the Luta-Livre German Individual Championships in the Weight Class +99 kg.

The Author
Christian Braun has been practicing various forms of martial arts for 20 years. Since 1996, he has concentrated on the system and methods in FMA. He has learned from experts like Paul Vunak (Progressive Fighting Systems), Jeff Espinous and Johan Skalberg (International Kali Arnis Eskrima Federation), and possesses

instructor licenses for both organizations. In addition, he learned about weapons from Mike Inay and Bob Breen, as well as from many other experts. For several years he has instructed on national courses throughout Germany for the German Ju-Jutsu Association (Deutscher Ju-Jutsu Verband e.V.) and he also regularly carries out training for personal security guards. He is a Grand Master in Ju-Jutsu (5th Dan), JJ-Instructor and Trainer 'B' License. He is also the holder of further Master titles in traditional Jiu-Jitsu systems.

Books Published:
See Literature

DVD Published:
See DVDs

Photo & Illustration Credits

Cover Design:	Sabine Groten
Cover Photo:	Imago Sportfotodienst GmbH
Photos inside:	Christian Braun and Gabriele Rogall-Zelt